CW00411090

SCARBOROUGH'S MEMBERS OF PARLIAMENT
1832 to 1906

SCARBOROUGH'S MAYORS
1836 to 1906

A
BIOGRAPHICAL DICTIONARY

by

ANNE & PAUL BAYLISS

SCARBOROUGH'S MEMBERS OF PARLIAMENT
1832 to 1906
SCARBOROUGH'S MAYORS
1836 to 1906

A BIOGRAPHICAL DICTIONARY

by

ANNE & PAUL BAYLISS

© 2008 A.M. BAYLISS
ISBN 0 9506405 7 3

The authors assert the moral right to be identified as the authors of this work.

All rights reserved. No part of this book may be reproduced or transmitted in any form or by any means, electronic or mechanical, including photocopying, recording or by information storage and retrieval systems, without prior written permission of the publishers, except in the case of brief quotations embodied in critical articles and reviews.

The information contained in this book is as accurate as the sources used have permitted. However, the publishers do not accept any responsibility for any errors or omissions present in the text.

This book is therefore sold as is, without warranty of any kind, express or implied, respecting its contents, including, but not limited to implied warranties for the book's quality, performance, merchantability or fitness for any particular purpose. Neither the publishers nor their dealers or distributors shall be liable to the purchaser or any other person or entity with respect to any liability, loss or damage caused, or alleged to be caused directly or indirectly by this book.

Published by
A.M. Bayliss
2, Cooks Gardens,
Scalby,
North Yorks YO13 0SU

CONTENTS

Scarborough Constitutional (Conservative) Club opened 1888

ALSO BY THE AUTHORS

Scarborough Hospital and Dispensary
The First Fifty Years 1852-1902
by
Anne & Paul Bayliss and Alan Jackson
ISBN 0 09506405 6 5
The Medical Profession in Scarborough 1700-1899
A Biographical Directory
by
Anne & Paul Bayliss
ISBN 0 9506405 5 7
Architects and Civil Engineers of Nineteenth Century Scarborough
by
Anne & Paul Bayliss
ISBN 0 9506405 4 9
Photographers in Mid Nineteenth Century Scarborough
by
Anne & Paul Bayliss
ISBN 0 9506405 3 0
Scarborough Artists of the Nineteenth Century
by
Anne & Paul Bayliss
ISBN 0 9506405 2 2
William James Boddy, York Artist (1832-1911),
His Life and Works
by
Anne & Paul Bayliss
ISBN 0 9506405 1 4
The Life and Works of James Trubshaw (1777-1853)
Staffordshire Builder, Architect and Civil Engineer
by
Anne Bayliss
ISBN 0 9506405 0 6
Sir Charles Wolseley (1769-1846)
The Radical Baronet
by
Anne Bayliss
ISBN 0 903363 20 8

FOREWORD

The subject of this biographical dictionary, MPs and Mayors of Scarborough, was suggested to us by the Town's reference librarian, Jon Webster, as a topic of public enquiry on which there was little, if any, organised information.

Jon Webster's suggestion was made in the context of the *Library Archives Group*. This is a small team of members of Scarborough Archaeological and Historical Society which meets each Thursday evening in Scarborough Library to assist staff with a range of projects relating to the Library's collection of historical material on Scarborough. The Group works under the general direction of retired reference librarian, Bryan Berryman. To date, projects tackled have included the cataloguing of the photograph collection and the postcard collection, the indexing of a collection of theatre programmes, the correlation of 19th century large scale maps with contemporary census returns, the transcription of old documents and deeds, the extraction of Scarborough data from standard Yorkshire volumes, the indexing of local history journals, research into the 19th century Scarborough printer and publisher, John Cole and research in to the suffragette movement in the Town.

The period that this dictionary covers begins with the reform of Parliamentary elections in 1832, for MPs, and municipal reform in 1836 for mayors and continues until 1906 although the MP elected for Scarborough in that year continued in office until 1918. This is a biographical dictionary rather than a history of national or local politics over the period covered. We have provided brief introductions to both sections to describe what came before the reforms of the 1830s but the reader seeking a political history needs to look further. All of the information used to compile entries in the dictionary has been found either in Scarborough Reference Library or via one of the online services that the Library offers. We have indicated our sources, where appropriate, at the end of each entry under the heading *Further reading*. Local directories and census records were also used but have not been listed under this heading.

We have, as far as possible, striven for accuracy in compiling the dictionary but there may still be errors of omission or commission in the book. We apologise to our readers for any such defaults that they find and we hope they will bring them to our attention so they may be rectified, at least in our data base.

Anne & Paul Bayliss
January 2008

ACKNOWLEDGMENTS

All of the sources used in the compilation of this book are to be found in the historical reference collection of Scarborough Library or can be accessed via the on-line services that the Library provides.

We would like to thank North Yorkshire County Library and Information Services for making this material freely available to us and specifically to Jon Webster and Bryan Berryman for tracking down the more obscure pieces of information that we sought.

We also thank North Yorkshire County Library and Information Services for permission to use all of the illustrations in this dictionary. The quality of these illustrations varies but on occasions we have felt that it was better to include a poor quality portrait than none at all.

We also wish to thank Peter Robson for nuggets of information on the Rowntree family and on Thomas Whittaker and also the Mayor's Secretary, Irene Webster, for tracking down George Willis's date of death and for

providing us with a list of portraits in the Town Hall.

Electioneering in Scarborough 4 July 1892

SCARBOROUGH'S
MEMBERS OF PARLIAMENT
1832 to 1906

INTRODUCTION

From the eleventh century, the Borough of Scarborough had the privilege of sending two members to Parliament. These men were not elected by the freeholders of the Town but by the 44 members of the Old Corporation made up of two bailiffs, two coroners, four chamberlains and a common council of 36, divided into three benches of twelve each. The system in Scarborough had been challenged twice during the 18th century. In 1736, the Corporation and the Borough Freemen supported different candidates. The Freemen's candidate was successful but the Corporation's defeated candidate petitioned the House of Commons which decided that only the Corporation votes should count and overturned the result. The next challenge came in 1791 when Parliament decided in favour of the householders but in the contested election of 1802 only 33 bothered to vote. There were nine further elections in Scarborough up to and including 1831, all uncontested.

At the beginning of the 19th century Scarborough, like many other ancient towns, was a *pocket borough* i.e. a constituency where the choice of the member of Parliament was in the hands of a rich and powerful family whose wealth and influence with the Corporation ensured that their favoured candidate was always elected unopposed. In Scarborough, the Duke of Rutland and his family controlled one seat and the Earls of Mulgrave the other. From 1806 to 1832, the Rutland seat was held by Charles Manners Sutton (1780-1845), eldest son of the Archbishop of Canterbury. The Mulgrave seat was held by Edmund Phipps from 1796 to 1820 when he became Viscount Normanby, and then his son. the Hon. Edmund Phipps, held the seat until 1832.

Reform of the electoral system throughout the country was long overdue but was fiercely resisted by those Parliamentarians whose seats depended on patronage in the *rotten and pocket boroughs*. After much opposition to any change, the Great Reform Act (Representation of the People Act) 1832 was passed by Parliament. This gave the franchise to all adult males who were owners or tenants of property worth £10 or more. Scarborough kept its two seats in Parliament but now the right of the Old Corporation to elect the members was finally removed. This was a fatal blow to the Rutland

1

and Mulgrave patronages.

At the first general election after the Reform Act, held in 1832, the two sitting members for Scarborough, Manners Sutton and Phipps, refused to stand. They realised that their association with the old regime would not help their election. Three candidates put up for the two Scarborough seats, for the Tories, the soldier Sir Frederick Trench (q.v.) and for the Whigs, Sir George Cayley (q.v.) and Sir John Johnstone (q.v.), both of whom were local and respected landowners who had supported reform. The votes cast were Johnstone 296, Cayley 265 and Trench 209. Johnstone and Cayley were thus elected, beginning a long period of predominantly Liberal politics in Scarborough.

The Borough of Scarborough's two seat status continued until the Seats Redistribution Act 1884, which reduced the number to one. In 1918, the seat was abolished and the constituency became the Scarborough and Whitby Division of North Yorkshire.

Further reading
Binns, Jack, The History of Scarborough, North Yorkshire, Blackthorn Press, 2003 Chapter 12 (Politics)
Hinderwell, Thomas, The History and Antiquities of Scarborough 3rd edition 1832 pgs 132-145 (Parliamentary history prior to reform)

Advertisements.

LIBERAL ELECTORS!

What does the cry of a United Liberal Party mean ?
The MONOPOLY of both the seats by the Whig section of the party.
What does "dividing the Liberal Party" mean ?
Giving the Working Class and Nonconformist Electors, who are the great majority, their FAIR share in the representation.
It is a sham to talk of a United Liberal Party so long as the great majority of Liberals are practically unrepresented.
If you want Religious Equality; the Repeal of the Criminal Law Amendment Act; the Abolition of the Game Laws; National and NOT Denominational Education; and an end to all unjust Class Legislation

PLUMP FOR
THOROLD ROGERS.
The People's Candidate and the truest Liberal.
P.S.—He will not Alter HIS Opinions to keep his seat.

Scarborough Free Lance, 31 January 1874

2

CHRONOLOGICAL LIST
of SCARBOROUGH MPs
1832-1906

TWO SEAT CONSTITUENCY

1832 General Election

Sir John Johnstone	Whig	296
Sir George Cayley	Whig	265
Sir Frederick Trench	Tory	209	defeated

This was the first general election after the Great Reform Act of 1832. The Whigs won a large majority, the Tories taking less than 30% of the vote.

1835 General Election

Sir Frederick Trench	Tory	176
Sir John Johnstone	Whig	161
Sir George Cayley	Whig	122	defeated

The Whigs maintained their majority but the Tories under Robert Peel made considerable gains.

1837 General Election

Sir Frederick Trench	Tory	225
Sir Thomas Style	Whig	211
Sir John Johnstone	Whig	192	defeated

The Whigs maintained their majority but the Tories made even further gains

1841 General Election

Sir John Johnstone	Whig	296
Sir Frederick Trench	Tory	253
Hon. Charles B. Phipps	Whig	237	defeated

The Tories took control under Robert Peel.

1847 General Election

Sir John Johnstone	Whig	(unopposed)
Earl Mulgrave	Whig	(unopposed)

The Tories, now referred to as Conservatives, won most of the seats but a split appeared in their ranks between those supporting free-trade and the protectionists.

3

1851 Scarborough by-election (July)

*Earl Mulgrave was required to seek re-election having been appointed
Comptroller of the Household but was defeated.*

George F. Young	Tory	314	
Earl Mulgrave	Whig	281	defeated

1852 General Election

Sir John Johnstone	Whig	422	
Earl Mulgrave	Whig	387	
George F. Young	Tory	313	defeated

*The conservatives won a slight majority over the Whigs. Attempts to form
a majority government failed and a coalition ensued.*

1857 General Election

Sir John Johnstone	Whig	540	
Earl Mulgrave	Whig	508	
Dr Aug. F. Bayford	Tory	275	defeated

The Whigs, under Lord Palmerston, won a majority.

1857 Scarborough by-election (December)

*By-election caused by appointment of Earl Mulgrave as Lieutenant
Governor of Nova Scotia.*

John Dent Dent	Whig	373	
George John Cayley	Tory	280	defeated

1859 General Election

Hon. W. H. F. Denison	Whig	562	
Sir John Johnstone	Whig	540	
John Dent Dent	Whig	428	defeated
George John Cayley	Tory	65	defeated

*The Liberals, into which party the Whigs had been assimilated, maintained
their majority.*

1860 Scarborough by-election

*By-election caused by William Denison succeeding to the Peerage as
Baron Londesborough.*

John Dent Dent	Liberal	472	
Lieut. Col. Caulfield	Con.	340	defeated

1865 General Election

Sir John Johnstone	Liberal	932	
John Dent Dent	Liberal	674	
George John Cayley	Con.	441	defeated

The Liberals increased their large majority.

1868 General Election

Sir John Johnstone	Liberal	1,826	
John Dent Dent	Liberal	1,678	
George John Cayley	Con.	742	defeated

The Liberals further increased their majority. This was the first election after the Reform Act 1867 which, amongst other reforms, enfranchised every male adult householder living in a borough constituency and also male lodgers paying £10 for unfurnished property, giving the vote to about 1.5 million men.

1869 Uncontested Scarborough by-election

By-election caused by the death of Sir John Johnstone. However, his son Sir Harcourt Johnstone was returned unopposed.

Sir Harcourt Johnstone	Liberal unopposed

1874 General Election

Sir Charles Legard	Con.	1,280	
Sir Harcourt Johnstone	Liberal	1,103	
John Dent Dent	Liberal	799	defeated
Prof. J. E. Thorold Rogers	Liberal	772	defeated

The conservatives won a majority of seats. This was the first election following the Secret Ballot Act 1872. One result of this was the election of Irish Nationalists whose supporters could now cast their votes without the scrutiny of their landlords.

1880 General Election (April)

Sir Harcourt Johnstone	Liberal	2,157	
William Sproston Caine	Liberal	2,065	
Lieut.-Col. Fife-Cookson	Con.	1,581	defeated
Sir Charles Legard	Con.	1,562	defeated

The Liberals won one of their largest majorities.

1880 Scarborough by-election (July)

By-election caused by Sir Harcourt Johnstone being raised to the Peerage as Baron Derwent.

Rt. Hon. J. G. Dodson	Liberal	1,828	
Arthur Duncombe	Con.	1,606	defeated

1884 By-election (3 November)
By-election caused by elevation of John Dodson to the Peerage as Baron Monk-Breton.
Lieut. - Col. Steble   Liberal 1,895
Sir George R. Sitwell   Con.   1,606 defeated

1884 Scarborough by-election (26 November)
W. S. Caine was required to seek re-election having being appointed Lord of the Admiralty.
William S. Caine   Liberal 1,832
Sir George R. Sitwell   Con.   1,639 defeated

ONE SEAT CONSTITUENCY

1885 General Election
Sir George R. Sitwell   Con.   2,185
John Glover   Liberal 2,047 defeated
The Liberals won most seats but not an overall majority, the Irish Nationalists holding the balance of power. This was the first election after the Reform Act 1884 which increased the electorate to about 5.7 million males. It also abolished most two member constituencies, including Scarborough.

1886 General Election
Joshua Rowntree   Liberal 2,122
Sir George R. Sitwell   Con.   2,020 defeated
The Conservatives, in coalition with the Unionist wing of the Liberal Party, won a majority. The election was called because the hung Parliament following the 1885 election had opened up splits in the Liberal Party over home rule for Ireland.

1892 General Election
Sir George R. Sitwell   Con.   2,293
Joshua Rowntree   Liberal 2,122 defeated
The Conservatives won the most seats but not a majority. The Liberals had won more seats than in 1886 and formed a minority government with the support of the Irish Nationalists.

1895 General Election
J. Compton Rickett   Liberal 2,415
Sir George R. Sitwell   Con.   2,391 defeated
The Conservatives won a large majority.

1900 General Election
Sir Compton Rickett   Liberal 2,548
Sir George R. Sitwell   Con.   2,441   defeated
The Conservatives won a large majority including 163 uncontested seats. This was the first election in which candidates from the Labour Representation Committee, later the Labour Party, stood.

1906 General Election
Walter R. Rea   Liberal 3,128
Charles E. Hunter   Con.   2,619   defeated
The Liberals took a huge majority and the Conservatives lost over half their seats. The Labour Party won 29 seats.

Walter Rea continued to represent Scarborough in Parliament until 1918 being returned in two elections in 1910

1910 General Election (February)
Walter R. Rea   Liberal 3,011
G. Monckton-Arundell Con.   2,719   defeated
The result was a hung Parliament and a further general election was held in the same year.

1910 General Election (December)
Walter R. Rea   Liberal 2,763
G. Monckton-Arundell Con.   2,711   defeated
The result was still a hung Parliament but the Liberals formed a Government with the support of the Irish Nationalists.

SCARBOROUGH'S MEMBERS
of
PARLIAMENT
1832 to 1906

THE DICTIONARY

CAINE, William Sproston
1842 (Cheshire) - 1903 (London)
Scarborough MP (Liberal) 1880 - 1885

William Sproston Caine was born on 26 March 1842 at Egremont on the Wirral Peninsula. He was the son of Hannah and Nathanial Caine J.P., a metal merchant. William Caine was educated at two nearby private schools. In 1861, he entered his father's business and became a partner in 1864 and, although he moved to Liverpool in 1871, he continued to work in the family business. His father died in 1877 and William resigned the following year. He had directorships of other businesses and acquired a controlling interest in  *Shaw's Brow Iron Company* in Liverpool but left the management to a junior partner. The company collapsed in 1893 leaving Caine with a considerable debt which he eventually managed to pay off.

In 1862, during his travels on business, he came across *Haste to the Rescue,* a temperance tract by the activist Julia Wightman (1817-1898) and he immediately took a pledge of abstinence from alcohol. For the rest of his life he involved himself in every aspect of the Temperance Movement and it was in furtherance of this that he took up politics.

W. S. Caine had stood for Parliament as a Liberal candidate for Liverpool but had twice been unsuccessful. In 1877, he was persuaded to come to Scarborough by fellow Liberal and temperance campaigner, Joshua Rowntree (q.v.), with a view to being the second Liberal candidate alongside Sir Harcourt Johnstone (q.v.) for the 1880 general election.

Caine's first address to the electors of Scarborough was on 4 December 1877. In 1878, he and his family moved to Scarborough and he was responsible for reorganising the local Liberal Party. From the start of his electioneering, Caine refused to subscribe to institutions such as churches, bazaars, cricket and football clubs etc to avoid accusations of influencing the voters. He did, however, lay a principal foundation stone for the Falsgrave Primitive Methodist Chapel in September 1879. Together with fellow Liberal Sir Harcourt Johnstone, Caine was successful in the April 1880 general election, the unsuccessful Conservative candidates being Sir Charles Legard (q.v.) and Lieutenant Colonel Fife-Cookson. Although, as an MP, Caine moved to London, he remained active in Scarborough, giving lectures on a range of subjects and involving himself in many public events in the Town. In 1882, he laid one of the main foundation stones for Scarborough's new Salvation Army Barracks. It was almost entirely due to the efforts of W. S. Caine that Scarborough School of Art was founded in 1882 and he was also a strong supporter in the Town of the University Extension Movement and the Adult School Movement. He was a magistrate for the North Riding of Yorkshire and also for the County of London. In 1884, Caine was appointed Civil Lord of the Admiralty, which required him to stand for re-election and he was successful at the ensuing by-election in Scarborough on 26 November 1884, his opponent being the Conservative, Sir George Sitwell, Bart. (q.v.).

In 1885, Scarborough's representation in Parliament was reduced from two MPs to one and Caine did not stand again for election in the Town. He had been persuaded to stand for Middlesex, which, by the Seats Redistribution Act, was divided into two. Caine stood for Tottenham, one of these divisions, but was defeated. In 1886, he was returned for Barrow and converted to Liberal Unionism. In 1890, as a protest against a Parliamentary scheme to recompense publicans who licences were cancelled, he resigned his seat, re-joined the Liberal Party, offered himself for re-election but was defeated. In 1892, he was elected MP for Bradford but was defeated there in 1895. However, he was elected later in that year for Camborne, which constituency he represented until his death.

William Caine's public and Parliamentary career was dominated by two issues - temperance and India. He was a member of the Royal Commission on Licensing Laws and a senior member of almost every major temperance society in the country. He was President of the National Temperance Federation from its formation in 1864 and in London he was closely associated with the Wheatsheaf Mission Church. Caine visited India in 1890 as a delegate to the India National Congress in Calcutta and from 1895 to 1896 he was a member of the Royal Commission on Indian

Expenditure. He spoke against British methods of government there which, he claimed, used the sale of alcohol and opium for financial gain. He published a series of articles on India in some of which he advocated a degree of self-government.

William Caine was brought up as a Baptist and was much influenced by the Liverpool preacher and social reformer, Hugh Stowell Brown (1823-1886), whose reminiscences he edited for publication in 1887. On 24 March 1868 Caine had married Brown's daughter Alice. They had three daughters and two sons, one of the latter taking up practice at the Parliamentary Bar. In 1902, while MP for the Camborne Division of Cornwall, Caine's health broke down and he was ordered to take a prolonged voyage to South America. However, this did not improve his health and he died at his London home, Grosvenor Road, Westminster on 17 March 1903 aged 59. He was buried at Brookwood Cemetery, Woking.

Further Reading
Scarborough Mercury, Friday 20 March 1903 (Obituary)
Scarborough Pictorial 31 Dec 1913 (Biography)
Oxford Dictionary of National Biography
Bayliss A. & P., The Origins and First 25 years of Scarborough School of Art (1882-1907), Transactions of the Scarborough Archaeological and Historical Society, No. 35, pgs 18-35, 1999 (Caine's role in the foundation of the Art School)
Newton, John, W. S. Caine MP – a Biography, James Nisbet & Co. Ltd, London 1907

CAYLEY, Sir George, Bart.
1773 (Scarborough) - 1857 (Brompton Hall)
Scarborough (Whig) MP 1832-1835

George Cayley was born at Paradise House, Scarborough on 27 December 1773. He was the only son of Sir Thomas Cayley (1732-1792) and his wife Isabella Sewton. Sir Thomas was the fifth Baronet of Brompton, a village eight miles South-West of Scarborough. George Cayley was educated by two non-conformist ministers - George Walker FRS of Nottingham and George Cadogan Morgan of Southgate, Middlesex. In 1792, Sir Thomas died, George Cayley inherited the family estates, became the sixth Baronet and moved to Brompton Hall.

Cayley was very much a child of the *English Enlightenment* involving himself with a large number of scientific and technological areas to all of

which he made significant contributions.
In 1800, he took a leading part in getting
an Act of Parliament for the Muston
Drainage Scheme. The aim was to drain
about 10,000 acres of frequently flooded
land West of Scarborough, between the
Rivers Derwent and Hertford. The
engineer for the project was William
Chapman (1749-1832) and Cayley was
chairman. Cayley also took a great
interest in aeronautics. From 1799, he
developed the concept of a fixed wing
aircraft and was experimenting with a
glider from as early as 1809. However,
it was not until 1853 that he had built a
full size one, said to have been flown by
his coachman. Cayley's other ideas, projects and publications included a
caterpillar tractor, railway systems and the design of projectiles. For one of
his tenants he even designed an artificial arm. He was President of York
Mechanics' Institute from its foundation and was a founder member of the
Yorkshire and the Scarborough Philosophical Societies and of the British
Association, which first met in York in 1831. He was involved in the
foundation of the Royal Polytechnic Institution (now the University of
Westminster) and was its Chairman for many years.

Presumably influenced by his two non-conformist teachers, Sir George
Cayley became an active advocate of Parliamentary and later, municipal
reform. He was President of the York Whig Club from 1821 to 1827, the
most influential reformist institution in the North of England. After the
Reform Act of 1832, Cayley agreed to stand for one of Scarborough's two
Parliamentary seats and, together with his Whig colleague Sir J.V.B
Johnstone (q.v.), he was elected. However, with the fall of the Whig
Government in 1834, there was another general election in January 1835
and although Cayley stood again for Scarborough, he lost his seat to Sir
Frederick Trench (q.v.). Cayley was a Borough magistrate for
Scarborough.

George Cayley married Sarah, the daughter of George Walker, one of his
two teachers, and they had three sons and seven daughters. Lady Sarah
Cayley died in 1854 and Sir George died three years later at Brompton Hall
on 15 December 1857, twelve days before his 84th birthday. He was buried
in the family vault under the chancel of Brompton Parish Church. He was
succeeded by his son Digby who became the 7th Baronet.

Further Reading

Scarborough Mercury 15 December 1857 (Obituary)

Oxford Dictionary of National Biography

Binns, Jack, Heroes, Rogues and Eccentrics, A Biographical Journey Through Scarborough's Past, Blackthorn Press, 2002 pgs 165-174

Fairlie, G. & Cayley, Elizabeth, The Life of a Genius, 1965, Hodder & Stoughton

Gibbs-Smith, Charles H., Sir George Cayley's Aeronautics, 1796-1855, HMSO 1962

Pritchard, J. Laurence, First Cayley Memorial Lecture 4 November 1952, Sir George Cayley, Bart. The Father of British Aeronautics, the Man and his Work. Royal Aeronautical Society

DENISON, William Henry Forester
(Later Lord Londesborough and Viscount Raincliffe)
1834 - 1900 (London)

Scarborough MP (Whig) 1859

William Henry Forester Denison was born on 19 June 1834, the eldest son of Lord Albert Conyngham and his first wife Henrietta Mary Weld-Forester. Having succeeded to property of his uncle, William Joseph Denison, MP for Surrey, Lord Albert assumed, by Royal Licence, the surname Denison. He was then elevated to the peerage as Baron Londesborough in 1850. He was a large landowner with property amounting to almost 70,000 acres with £100,000 rental value at the time of his death in 1860, including estates around Scarborough at Seamer, East Ayton, Deepdale and Throxenby.

William Henry Forrester Denison was educated at Eton and in 1857 was elected Liberal Member of Parliament for Beverley in the East Riding of Yorkshire. However, the Beverley election had been costly and as it was an expensive seat to retain. Denison decided to put himself forward as a Liberal candidate for Scarborough and in 1859 he, together with Sir John Johnstone (q.v.), was elected. However, Denison only served nine months as the Town's MP because his father died in 1860 and he was elevated to the House of Lords as the Second Baron Londesborough. Thereafter he did not take a very active role in politics. He left the Liberal Party over the question of home rule for Ireland. He joined the Conservatives and became Chairman of the Board of Directors of Scarborough Constitutional (Conservative) Club. In 1887, Queen Victoria's jubilee year, while he was President of the National Union of Conservative Associations, an Earldom was conferred on him, the only peer thus honoured. He became Viscount Raincliffe, of Raincliffe in the North Riding, and Earl of Londesborough, in the County of York.

In September 1863, Denison, then Baron Londesborough, married Lady Edith Frances Wilhelmina Somerset, the youngest daughter of the 7th Duke of Beaufort. The Mayor of Scarborough, Godfrey Knight (q.v.), organised a public procession in the Town to welcome his Lordship and his bride to their house, *Londesborough Lodge*, in the Crescent. This was said to be the most extensive demonstration that had ever taken place in the Town. The procession included fishermen and sailors carrying banners, local tenants of the Londesboroughs mounted on horseback, the band of the 6th North Yorks Rifles, the Artillery Corps, the Rifle Corps and representatives of the Town Council and of local Friendly Societies. Formal addresses were presented to and acknowledged by his Lordship.

Scarborough's welcome for the couple was generously repaid by Lord Londesborough who became a familiar figure on the streets of the Town. He was a major promoter of Scarborough Cricket Club and its annual festival. His financial support, together with that of Sir Harcourt Johnstone (q.v.) and Sir Charles Legard (q.v.), the three original trustees of the Club, meant that it could buy the freehold of the cricket ground from the Woodall family in 1877. Londesborough provided hospitality for the gentlemen players and kept a house in the Crescent exclusively for the use of cricketers. Lord Londesborough was generous with his support for the tennis carnival and, being keen on sailing, tried to establish a regatta in the Town. He was a breeder and judge of horses and laid out a racecourse on Seamer Moor. However, this was not a success as a rowdy element was said to have infiltrated it and it was later used as a camping ground for the Volunteers. Londesborough was active in field sports but after he lost the sight of one eye in an accident he was barred from further shooting.

The Londesboroughs entertained many notable guests at their Scarborough house, which helped to maintain the reputation of the Town as *Queen of Watering Places*. The Prince of Wales was their guest on three occasions, in November 1869, in November 1870 and in October 1871 when he was accompanied by the Princess of Wales. After this visit the Prince developed typhoid fever which was attributed to his stay at *Londesborough Lodge*. However, many believed that it had been contracted at

Sandringham, where a groom, who had never visited Scarborough, had died of typhoid. Later royal visitors to *Londesborough Lodge* included the Duke of Cambridge and the Duke and Duchess of Teck.

Lord Londesborough was Vice-Admiral of the Yorkshire Coast, Honorary Colonel of the 4th East Yorkshire Artillery Volunteers and Lieutenant Colonel of the 1st West Yorkshire Royal Volunteers.

Lord and Lady Londsborough had five children, four daughters and one son - Edith, Lilian, Ida, Mildred and William. Lady Edith Denison (died 1945) married Sir Gerald Codrington, Bart., Lady Lilian Denison married Newton Charles Ogle of Kirkley in 1895 but died in 1899, Lady Mildred Denison (died 1953) married Sir William Cooke, Bart. and Lady Ida Denison (died 1937) married Sir George Sitwell, Bart. (q.v.). Sir William Denison, born 1864, married Lady Grace Fane, daughter of the Earl of Westmoreland.

William Henry Forester Denison, the First Earl of Londesborough and Viscount Raincliffe, died on Thursday 19 April 1900 at his London residence in Grosvenor Square, at the age of 65. His widow, Edith, Lady Londesborough, died in 1915. His son, William, succeeded as Second Earl Londesborough but died in 1917 at the age of 52.

Further reading
Scarborough Mercury, Friday 20 April 1900 (Obituary)
Scarborough Pictorial 6 August 1913 (Son)
Scarborough Pictorial 28 January 1914 pg 7 (Biography)
Scarborough Pictorial 21 January 1914 (The Barony of Londesborough)
Binns, Jack, Heroes, Rogues and Eccentrics, A Biographical Journey Through Scarborough's Past, Blackthorn Press, 2002 pgs 183-189 (Baron Albert and the Denisons)
Blakey, J.W. (ed.) Some Scarborough Faces, Past and Present, Scarborough Gazette Printing & Publishing Co. 1901 pgs 60-63 (Biography)
Hall, Ian & Found, John, Cricket at Scarborough, a Social History of the Club and its Festival, Breedon Books Sport, 1992

DENT, John Dent
1826 (Doncaster) – 1894 (Wetherby)
Scarborough MP (Whig) 1857-1859 & 1860-1874

John Dent Dent, born on 11 June 1826, was the eldest son of Joseph Tricket who, in 1834, assumed the name Dent when he inherited property from his uncle, Jonathan Dent of Winterton, Lincs. Joseph Dent then

bought the Ribston estate near Wetherby. John Dent Dent was educated at Eton and Trinity College, Cambridge, graduating with a BA in 1848 and MA in 1851. He was called to the Bar at Lincoln's Inn but opted for a Parliamentary career. He joined the Whig Party and in 1852 he was elected MP for Knaresborough. In 1857, a by-election was caused in Scarborough by the resignation of George, Earl Mulgrave (q.v.). Dent was accepted as the Liberal candidate and was elected, his Conservative opponent being Sir George Cayley (q.v.). In the 1859 election in Scarborough, when there were two further Liberal candidates, Sir John Johnstone (q.v.) and William Denison (q.v.), Dent was defeated. However, in 1860, Denison was elevated to the House of Lords and Dent was successful in the resulting by-election. He was re-elected for Scarborough in 1865 and in 1868 and held the seat until the election of 1874. On that occasion there were three Liberal candidates, Dent, Sir Harcourt Johnstone (q.v.) and Professor J. Thorald Rogers. The entry of the latter split the Liberal vote in the Town and Dent and Rogers were both defeated allowing the Conservative, Sir Charles Legard (q.v.) to be elected. The following year, 1875, Dent's father died and Dent inherited the family estates and did not enter Parliament again.

In 1879, John Dent Dent was elected a director of the North Eastern Railway Company, later becoming Chairman of the Board, a post he held until his death. He was also a director of the Forth Bridge Company to which the NE Railway subscribed. Dent was at various times a Trustee and Vice Chairman of the Royal Bath Hospital at Harrogate, a magistrate and a Deputy-Lieutenant for the West Riding of Yorkshire. He was a keen cricketer and a huntsman.

John Dent Dent married Mary Hebden, daughter of John Woodall (q.v.) on 10 July 1855 at St Mary's Church, Scarborough. They had four sons and three daughters. John Dent Dent died at Ribston Hall on 22 December 1894 and was buried at the local church at Hunsingore. His wife, Mary, survived him. His eldest son, Major J. W. Dent of the 4th Dragoon Guards was with his Regiment in India at the time of his father's death.

Further reading
Scarborough Mercury Friday 28 December 1894 (Obituary)

Scarborough Pictorial 25 March 1914 (Biography)
Blakey, J.W. (ed.) Some Scarborough Faces, Past and Present, Scarborough Gazette Printing & Publishing Co. 1901 pgs 80-82 (Biography)
Tomlinson, Wm. Weaver, North Eastern Railway, Andrew Reid & Co., Newcastle-on-Tyne, 1914 (History of North Eastern Railway)

DODSON John George
(Later Baron Monk-Breton)
1825 (London) - 1897 (London)
Scarborough MP (Liberal) 1880-1884

John George Dodson was born on 18 October 1825 in Mayfair, London, the only son of Sir John Dodson (1780-1858), a lawyer and judge and Frances née Pearson. J. G. Dodson was educated at Eton where he won the Prince Consort's Prize for modern languages and for the rest of his life was an acknowledged linguist. Dodson studied at Christ Church College, Oxford and graduated with a BA degree in 1847 (1st class in classics) and an MA degree in 1851. From 1847 to 1853 he travelled widely in the East, the Mediterranean and the USA. He wrote an account of his three month visit to Cyprus in 1848-49 which was included in *Murray's Handbook* until 1872. Dodson  visited the Crimea during the War. A mountaineer, he was a member of the Alpine Club and wrote several accounts of his climbs. In 1853, he was called to the Bar at Lincoln's Inn but opted for a Parliamentary career.

In 1852 and again in March 1857, Dodson unsuccessfully contested a seat in East Sussex as a Liberal. However, he was successful in April 1857 and held the seat until February 1874. In 1874 he was elected MP for the City of Chester and re-elected in the general election of 1880. In the same year he was appointed President of the Local Government Board in Gladstone's government, which required him to offer himself for re-election. Although successful in the ensuing by-election, his earlier election was declared void because of irregularities by his Liberal agents. Although his second election of that year was judged to be valid, he could neither sit nor vote in Parliament. This was clearly a problem for a minister of Gladstone's government. In July 1880, Sir Harcourt Johnstone (q.v.), the sitting member for Scarborough, stood down so that Dodson might be returned in the ensuing by-election. There were many local protests that the Borough was being made a convenience. The Conservatives were determined to oppose Dodson choosing Arthur Duncombe, the second son of the Hon. Admiral Duncombe as their candidate. However, Dodson was elected. Shortly after this, Harcourt Johnstone was raised to the peerage. John Dodson remained MP for Scarborough until 1884 when he was created a peer, becoming Baron Monk Breton of Conyboro and Hurstpierpoint, in Sussex. During his Parliamentary career Dodson was at various times Deputy Speaker, Financial Secretary to the Treasury, Chairman of the Public Accounts Committee, President of the Local Government Board and Chancellor of the Duchy of Lancaster. He was also an acknowledged authority on Parliamentary procedure. After being raised to the peerage, Dodson took no further part in national politics but was appointed the first chairman of East Sussex County Council (1889-1892).

John George Dodson married Florence, the second daughter of William J. Campion of Danny, Sussex in January 1856. They had one son and three daughters. Dodson died on 25 May 1897 in London and was buried in Barkham Church on his estate. At the time of his death his estate was valued at almost £136,000. His wife, Florence, died on 17 February 1912. J. G. Dodson was succeeded by his only son John William Dodson.

Further reading
Scarborough Pictorial 10 December 1913 (Sir Harcourt Johnstone's role in Dodson's election)
Oxford Dictionary of National Biography

JOHNSTONE, Sir Harcourt
(Later Baron Derwent of Hackness)
1829 (Bishopthorpe, York) - 1916 (Hackness Hall, nr Scarborough)
Scarborough MP (Liberal) 1869-1880

Harcourt Johnstone was born on 3 January 1829 at Bishopthorpe, the official residence of the Archbishop of York. Harcourt was the eldest son of Sir John V. B. Johnstone (q.v.) and his wife Louisa Augusta, daughter of the Most Reverend Edward Harcourt, Archbishop of York. After being educated at Eton College, Harcourt Johnstone served in the Second Life Guards. In 1869, he resigned his commission on the death of his father who had been Liberal MP for Scarborough since 1841. Harcourt immediately stood as the Liberal candidate in the resulting by-election and was returned unopposed.

In the 1874 election, Harcourt Johnstone retained his seat for Scarborough and was again successful in the general election of April 1880. However, in July of that year, he resigned in order to provide a safe seat for John Dodson (q.v.), a member of Gladstone's administration who had been unseated at Chester because of irregularities by his agents at the April general election. There were many local protests that the Borough was being made a convenience and the Conservatives determined to oppose Dodson by putting up Arthur Duncombe as their candidate. However, Dodson was elected in the ensuing Scarborough by-election. Sir Harcourt Johnstone was created the First Baron Derwent of Hackness in September 1881 in thanks for resigning his seat in Scarborough.

Sir Harcourt Johnstone involved himself with a range of activities in and around Scarborough. Together with William Denison (q.v.) (Lord Londesborough) and Sir Charles Legard (q.v.), Johnstone was one of the three original trustees of Scarborough Cricket Club who enabled it to buy the freehold of the cricket ground from the Woodall family in 1877. At various times Johnstone was Chairman of the Scarborough Board of Guardians, Chairman of the Local Highways Board and Chairman of the Royal Northern Sea-bathing Infirmary at Scarborough. From the 1850s until a week before his death, he was also a Scarborough Harbour Commissioner. Johnstone was elected a director of the North Eastern Railway Company in 1864 and in 1881, became Deputy Chairman until he resigned in 1888. He took a great interest in education and endowed the Lancasterian History Prize in the Town. He was a strong proponent of the establishment of a Free Library in Scarborough and offered £500 towards the purchase of a site. In fact such a library was not established in the Town until 1930. A magistrate and Deputy Lieutenant for the North Riding of Yorkshire, Sir Harcourt was a noted country gentleman and keen sportsman. He was, for many years, Master of the Hounds which hunted at Hackness. At the time of his death he owned 12,800 acres of land and was regarded as a very good landlord.

Harcourt Johnstone married Charlotte, daughter of Sir Charles Mills, Bart. on 2 May 1850. They had nine children; Francis the heir (1851-1929), Hilda (who died in infancy), Edward Henry (1854-1903) who became a planter in Ceylon, Cecil (1856-1833), Sir Alan (1858-1932), Edith (born 1860), the Hon. Louis (1862-1922), Mary (who died in infancy) and the Hon. Gilbert (1865-1949). Sir Alan V. B. Johnstone GCVO entered the diplomatic service in 1879 and was British Minister at The Hague and served in Vienna, Washington, Belgrade, Copenhagen and Rome.

Lady Derwent died on 22 August 1903. Although Lord Derwent had been in failing health for some years, he managed to attend the local Church on a regular basis. He died at Hackness Hall on 1 March 1916 and was succeeded by his eldest son Francis V. B. Johnstone.

Further Reading
Scarborough Pictorial 10 Dec 1913 (Family history)
Scarborough Mercury 3 March 1916 (Obituary)
Hall, Ian & Found, John, Cricket at Scarborough, a Social History of the Club and its Festival, Breedon Books Sport, 1992
Tomlinson, Wm. Weaver, North Eastern Railway, Andrew Reid & Co., Newcastle-on-Tyne, 1914 (History of North Eastern Railway)
Who's Who – Yorkshire, 1912, Westminster Publishing Co. Ltd London

JOHNSTONE, Sir John V. B.
1799 (Hackness) - 1869 (London)
Scarborough MP (Whig) 1832-1837 & 1841-1869

John Vanden Bempde Johnstone was born on 28 August 1799 at Hackness Hall, six miles North West of Scarborough. He was the son of Sir Richard Vanden Bempde Johnstone, 1st Baronet and his second wife, Margaret Scott. Sir Richard died in 1807 and John succeeded to the baronetcy at the age of seven. Sir John Johnstone was educated at Rugby School and at Trinity College, Cambridge, graduating in 1821.

Johnstone first entered Parliament in the autumn of 1830, when he was elected as a Whig for Yorkshire on the elevation of Lord Brougham to the peerage. Johnstone held this seat until the constituency was re-structured in 1832 under the Reform Act. He then stood as a candidate for Scarborough with fellow Whig Sir George Cayley (q.v.), both of whom had supported Parliamentary reform. The two previous Tory long-standing members for the Town, Charles Manners Sutton and Edmund Phipps refused to stand and their party's interest was represented by Sir Frederick Trench (q.v.). Johnstone headed the poll with 296 votes, Cayley was second with 265 votes and Trench was unsuccessful, receiving 209 votes. Johnstone was re-elected in 1835, lost his seat in 1837 but regained it in 1841 being re-elected thereafter until his death in 1869.

Altogether, Sir John Johnstone was MP for Scarborough for 33 years. His long tenure of one of Scarborough's two Parliamentary seats reflected the high esteem in which he was held in the Town. In 1827, he was one of the

19

principal founders of the Scarborough Philosophical Society and one year later he was one of the main movers in the establishment of the Rotunda Museum, the stone for which came from his Hackness Quarries. He also donated Hackness stone and gave other material support for the building of Christ Church, Scarborough, in 1828. Sir John was a Deputy Lieutenant of the North Riding of Yorkshire and Lieutenant Colonel of the West Riding Yeomanry. An owner of a considerable acreage of land, for many years he was an active member of the Council of the Royal Agricultural Society.

In 1825, Sir J. V. B. Johnstone married Louisa Augusta Venables-Vernon-Harcourt, daughter of the Right Reverend Dr Edward Harcourt, Archbishop of York and they had two sons and four daughters. Their elder son and heir was Harcourt Johnstone (q.v.) and their second son, Henry Richard (1830-1912) assumed the name Scott in 1860 on succeeding to estates at Woodall near Wetherby. Their daughters were Georgiana Emily (died 1863), Blanche Maria (died 1878), Elizabeth Margaret who married Sir Thomas Erskine Perry MP in 1855 and died 1913 and Caroline (1826-1892) who married Sir William Nevill, first Marquis of Abergavenny in 1848.

On Saturday 20 February 1869, Sir John V. B. Johnstone had an accident while hunting in the neighbourhood of London. His horse took an enormously high leap and threw him, and Sir John broke his collar bone and a rib. His son, Harcourt, immediately went to London, reporting back that his father's condition was serious but not dangerous. By Wednesday he was said to be perceptibly better but Sir John died the next day, 25 February, at 9-30am. His body was returned to Hackness where he was buried on 3 March 1869. Lady Johnstone survived her husband by less than half a year and died in August 1869.

Further Reading
Scarborough Mercury 27 February 1869 (Obituary)
Scarborough Pictorial 10 Dec 1913 (Family history and portrait above)
Baker, Joseph Brogden, The History of Scarborough, London, 1882 pgs 447-448 (Brief biography)

LEGARD, Sir Charles, Bart.
1846 (Ganton) - 1901 (Scarborough)
                                        Scarborough MP (Con.) 1874-1880

Charles Legard was born on 2 April 1846, the third son of Sir Thomas Digby Legard of Ganton (1803-1860), 8th Baronet and his wife Frances, daughter of Baron Feversham. Charles was educated at Eton College and served in the army as an ensign in the 43rd Light Infantry and was a Captain in the First West Riding Artillery Volunteer Corps. His eldest brother, Francis Digby Legard (1833-1865), inherited the baronetcy on the death of their father and when Francis died in Madeira, the eldest surviving brother, D'Arcy Widdrington Legard (1843-1866), inherited the title and estate. It was on the death of the latter, in Rome, in 1866, that Charles Legard inherited and became the 11th Baronet, whereupon he left the army to manage the estate lands and to follow a career in politics.

Sir Charles Legard's first public appearance in Scarborough was in October 1868 to preside at a meeting of the Town's Conservative Party. Legard was accepted as a Conservative candidate for a by-election in the City of Norwich in 1871 but there was public criticism of his involvement with *the turf* and he was defeated.   He was adopted as a Conservative candidate for Scarborough for the 1874 general election and set about an active reorganisation of the Party in the Town. He was returned to Parliament largely because the strong Liberal vote had been split by having three candidates. Legard began to take an active part in Parliamentary debates. He spoke against Sir Charles Trevelyan's motion to extend the franchise to the counties using, verbatim, a speech that George Canning had originally delivered before the advent of Parliamentary reform. This *faux-pas* was spotted by the *Scarborough Mercury* and caused Sir Charles much comment and notoriety. The fact that he again had horse-racing debts did not help his reputation.

By 1880 he was out of debt and again stood for Scarborough at the general election of that year, although many local Conservatives were very embarrassed by his candidature. There was considerable opposition to him and he was bottom of the poll, the two Liberal candidates, Harcourt Johnstone (q.v.) and W. S. Caine (q.v.) being returned.

Although Legard was later considered for other seats, he did not contest any constituency again. He did, however, continue to be very active in Scarborough politics, being elected President of the Town's Conservative Association on the death of Mr E. H. Hebden (q.v.) in 1880. In October 1893, Sir Charles was presented with a portrait of himself painted by Herman Gustave Herkomer, costing £270, subscribed to by 400 people in appreciation of his work for the local Association. In 1888, after the passing of the Local Government Act which created the County Councils, Legard was elected a member of the East Riding County Council, an Alderman and later Chairman of the Council. He was a Deputy Lieutenant and a Magistrate for the East Riding. He presided at Norton Police Court and was a Justice of the Peace for the North Riding of Yorkshire. In Scarborough he was elected to the Board of Guardians in 1895 after it had been re-constituted.

Legard was a member of the Scarborough Club from 1881. He was a patron of Scarborough Football Club and also a patron and trustee of Scarborough Cricket Club. Together with William Denison (q.v.) (Lord Londesborough) and Sir Harcourt Johnstone (q.v.), Legard was one of the three original trustees of the Club who enabled it to buy the freehold of the cricket ground from the Woodall family in 1877. Legard was President of the MCC from 1875-1876. On his Ganton estate he maintained a pack of otter hounds and a pack of harriers. Sir Charles Legard was a great friend of the Prince of Wales who he resembled and for whom he was often mistaken.

In November 1901, Sir Charles Legard was involved in an accident when he was thrown from his carriage. Early in December, while travelling to Scarborough he was taken ill. He consulted Dr Frederick Flint who recommended immediate rest and Sir Charles took a room at the Royal Hotel in the Town. Flint's diagnosis was of rheumatic fever. Sir Charles died of heart failure at the Hotel a few days later on 7 December 1901. When his body was taken from Scarborough to Ganton, crowds lined the route and an extra train was laid on to take mourners to the funeral. On Sir Charles's specific request he was buried in an ordinary grave in the burial ground of Ganton Church rather than in the family vault.

In February 1904, a memorial portrait of the late Sir Charles Legard, provided by public subscription, was formally presented to Scarborough Corporation at a meeting of the Town Council.

Sir Charles and Lady Legard had no children and the baronetcy and estate passed to Sir Charles's cousin, Algernon Willoughby Legard (1842-1923).

Further reading
Scarborough Mercury 13 December 1901 (Obituary)
Scarborough Pictorial 14 January 1914 (Biography)
Blakey, J.W. (ed.) Some Scarborough Faces, Past and Present, Scarborough Gazette Printing & Publishing Co. 1901 pgs 128-132 (Biography)
Hall, Ian & Found, John, Cricket at Scarborough, a Social History of the Club and its Festival, Breedon Books Sport, 1992 (History of Scarborough Cricket Club)

MULGRAVE, Earl
(George Phipps, later Second Marquis of Normanby)
1819 (London) - 1890 (Brighton)
Scarborough MP (Whig) 1847-1851 & 1852-1857

George Augustus Constantine Phipps was born on 23 July 1819, the only child of Constantine Henry Phipps, 1st Marquis of Normanby and his wife Maria Liddell, eldest daughter of Thomas Henry, Lord Ravensworth. The family seat was at Mulgrave Castle, near Lythe, a village four miles North-West of Whitby. The family owned much of the nearby land including the local alum works. George Phipps held the title Viscount Normanby from 1831 to 1838 and from 1838 to 1863 he was Earl Mulgrave. On his father's death in 1863, he became the second Marquis of Normanby.

In 1838, Earl Mulgrave had joined the Scots Fusilier Guards and in 1846 he was appointed a Major in the North Yorks Militia. However, in 1847, he resigned his commission to enter politics. In that year one of Scarborough's Tory MPs, Sir Frederick Trench (q.v.) resigned and in the ensuing by-election in July Earl Mulgrave was elected as a Liberal. He was appointed one of the Liberal Whips for Lord John Russell in the House of Commons. In 1851, he was appointed Comptroller of the Household which necessitated him putting himself up in the Borough for re-election. Mulgrave returned to Scarborough and spent several days canvassing in the Town. However, he supported free-trade which was unpopular with the townsfolk. A couple of days before the election a total stranger, George Young (q.v.), came to Scarborough to stand as a Tory protectionist. Young did not canvas the electorate but stated his principles and belief in trade protection. There were riots in the Town on the day of the election and, in spite of the longstanding connection between the Mulgrave family and Scarborough, George Young was elected with 314 votes to Mulgrave's 281. Earl Mulgrave accepted his defeat with bad grace.

Mulgrave stood again for Scarborough in the general election of 1852 and together with fellow Whig, Sir John Johnstone (q.v.), was elected to Parliament, this time defeating George Young. In this Parliament, Mulgrave served as a whip under Lord Aberdeen and Lord Palmerston. Mulgrave and Johnstone were both re-elected in the general election of 1857 but Mulgrave had to resign his seat the same year as he was appointed Lieutenant Governor of Nova Scotia. He held this office until July 1863 when he returned to England to succeed, on his father's death, as the second Marquis of Normanby. However, he later accepted a variety of overseas posts. He was Governor of Queensland in 1871, Governor of New Zealand in 1874 and Governor of Victoria from 1879 to 1884. In that year he returned to England as his wife was dying and he retired from public life on a pension. He had been created KCMG in 1874, GCMG in 1877 and GCB in 1885.

Earl Mulgrave married Laura, daughter of Captain Robert Russell RN on 17 August 1844 and she died on 26 January 1885. After a long illness, Mulgrave, now the Marquis of Normanby died at 6, Brunswick Terrace, Brighton on 3 April 1890. His body was brought back to be buried in St Oswald's Church, Lythe near Whitby. He was succeeded by his eldest son, Constantine Charles Henry, born 1846, who was Canon of Windsor from 1891 to 1907.

KCMG = Knight Commander of St Michael and St George
GCMG = Grand Cross of St Michael and St George
GCB = (Knight) Grand Cross of the Bath

Further reading
Yorkshire Gazette Saturday 26 July 1851 (1851 Scarborough election)
Oxford Dictionary of National Biography

REA, Walter Russell
(Later Baron Rea of Eskdale)
1873 (Liverpool) - 1948 (London)
Scarborough MP (Liberal) 1906-1918

Walter Russell Rea was born on 18 May 1873 in Liverpool, the son of Russell Rea MP, head of a firm of coal merchants and lighter-men with extensive Admiralty contracts. When Walter was eight, the family moved to Hampstead. Walter was educated at University College School and abroad. He entered his father's shipping firm and in due course became Chairman of the merchant banking business into which it developed.

Walter Rea's political life began when he was elected a member of Hampstead Borough Council. In November 1904, he was interviewed by the executive of Scarborough Liberal Association and was selected to represent the party in the Town. On 19 December 1905, Rea addressed his first public meeting in Scarborough, following his formal adoption as Liberal candidate. In 1906, he was elected with a majority of 509 votes against his Conservative opponent Charles Hunter, sharing in a national landslide to the Liberals.

The rejection of the Liberal Government's budget in 1909 by the House of Lords forced a general election in January/February 1910 which produced a hung Parliament. A further general election in December 1910 produced a similar result but the Liberal Party, under Herbert Asquith, formed a Government with the Irish Nationalists. The budget impasse with the House of Lords was resolved when the King agreed to created as many new peers as would be necessary to ensure its passage in that House. Walter Rea was elected member for Scarborough in both of the 1910 elections but with a much reduced majority of only 52 votes in the December election. The two general elections of 1910 were the last to span several days of voting.

Walter Rea continued to serve as the Town's MP until 1918 being its last Liberal member. A good speaker and staunch Free Trader, while member for Scarborough, Walter Rea was Junior Lord of the Treasury in both the Liberal government and under Herbert Asquith in the first coalition government of 1915-1916. In 1918, Rea stood unsuccessfully for Oldham and thereafter for a variety of constituencies, sometimes successfully, sometimes not. He represented Bradford North from 1923 to 1924 and

Dewsbury from 1931 to 1935, during which time he held office in the National Government of Ramsay Macdonald as Comptroller of the Household.

Walter Rea married Evelyn, the daughter of J. J. Muirhead, in 1896. After her death in 1930, he married Jemima, the daughter of Rev. Alexander Ewing in 1931. In 1935, Rea was created a Baronet and two years later he was made Baron Rea, of Eskdale in the County of Cumberland.

Lord Rea died in London on 26 May 1948, aged 74. At the time he was Honorary Treasurer of the Liberal Party. He was succeeded by Philip Rea, his eldest son from his first marriage, who became Liberal leader in the House of Lords.

Further reading
Scarborough Pictorial 20 August 1913 (Contemporary biography and portrait above)
Scarborough Evening News 27 May 1948 (Obituary)

RICKETT, Joseph Compton
1847 (London) - 1919 (Bournemouth)
                                    Scarborough MP (Liberal) 1895-1906

Joseph Compton Rickett was born on 13 February 1847 in London, the eldest son of Joseph Rickett of East Hoathly, Sussex. He was educated by private tutors and later at King Edward VI School at Bath, being the private pupil of the headmaster, Rev. Henry Stuart Fagan. Rickett took up a commercial career, becoming one of the principal proprietors of *Rickett, Smith & Co. Ltd.* of London, wholesale and retail coal merchants. He was also connected with several other London coal companies and was one of the principal owners of the *Sun Flour Mills Co. Ltd* of Bromley-by-Bow and Chelsea. He also owned considerable property in Sussex.

Rickett was adopted as Liberal candidate for Scarborough for the 1895 general election, being described at the time as an *eleventh hour choice*. This was his first foray into politics, his opponent being the sitting MP Sir George Sitwell (q.v.).

26

Sandwich boards supporting Rickett bore the slogan *Equal Treatment for Rich and Poor*, while Sitwell's displayed just a Union Jack. Rickett won by a small margin of 24 votes. Rickett was again elected in 1900, again against Sitwell but with a larger majority of 107 votes. In 1901, Rickett commissioned the Scarborough architects' firm, *Hall, Cooper & Davis*, to design a house for him - *Sea Croft*, Filey Road. Rickett did not fight the 1906 election for Scarborough but was elected for Osgoldcross, a seat he held until 1918, during which time he was Paymaster-General.

In 1868, Joseph Compton Rickett married Catherine Sarah, the second daughter of Rev. Henry J. Gamble of Upper Clapton, a very well-known congregational minister, and they had a large family. Rickett also became active in the Congregational Church movement and was appointed Chairman of the Congregational Union of England and Wales. He was also President of the National Council of Evangelical Free Churches. He was the author of several books including *Christ That is To Be* and *The Quickening of Caliban*.

Joseph Compton Rickett died on 30 July 1919 at Bournemouth.

Further reading
Scarborough Mercury 1 August 1919 (Obituary)
Blakey, J.W. (ed.) Some Scarborough Faces, Past and Present, Scarborough Gazette Printing & Publishing Co. 1901 pgs 100-102 (Biography)
Scott, W. Herbert, ed. W. T. Pike, North and East Ridings of Yorkshire Contemporary Biographies at the Opening of XX Century, Brighton 1903.

ROWNTREE, Joshua
1844 (Scarborough) - 1915 (Scalby)

Scarborough MP (Liberal) 1886-1892
Mayor 1885-1886

(This entry is repeated in the section on Mayors)

Joshua Rowntree, born on 6 April 1844, was the son of John and Jane Rowntree, Quaker grocers of Scarborough. In his early years Joshua, together with his sisters, was educated at home by a governess. He then went to Bootham School, a Quaker institution in York and later was articled to a solicitor in that City. After this he gained legal experience in London in the chambers of Sir E. Fry. In 1866, Rowntree returned to Scarborough to join the local solicitor, William Drawbridge, initially as a junior partner.

While in London, Joshua Rowntree had heard a speech by Earl Derby in the House of Lords. Derby had claimed that the declaration made by non-Anglican town councillors, that they would not injure the Establishment, was not worth the paper it was written on. Incensed by this, Rowntree joined the Liberation Society and thus began a life in Liberal politics. On his return to Scarborough, Rowntree was instrumental in the beginnings of adult education in the Town, a movement with which he was associated for the rest of his life. Scarborough's first Adult School was held in an old sail loft in Courtin Steps, Eastborough but grew rapidly and moved to larger premises in Spring Gardens in 1871 and then to new premises in St Sepulchre Street in 1894. The movement continued to grow and in 1903 Joshua Rowntree laid the foundation stone for the new Adult School in Roscoe Street. The movement included a rowing club which became Scarborough Rowing Club, a sick club and a Coffee Cart Company which became the Scarborough Coffee House Company (a temperance movement).

In 1868, Scarborough Council resolved to sell off the Old Town Hall in St Nicholas Street to a bank, a move resisted by many townsfolk. A committee was set up to oppose the sale and Joshua Rowntree was appointed secretary. The Local Government Board refused to approve the sale until after the November local elections of that year. The proposal was defeated when opponents were returned for the South and North Wards, and the building was converted into a public meeting room with shops below.

In 1878, Joshua Rowntree agreed to stand as a Liberal candidate for Scarborough Council, although he refused to canvass. He and William Barry (q.v.) were elected by a large majority to represent the South Ward. When Scarborough's two wards were divided into six, Rowntree stood as candidate for the East Ward but lost by just one vote. However, two months later a vacancy occurred in the same Ward and he was returned with a majority of 86. This was his last municipal contest. He was made Mayor of the Borough for the period 1885 to 1886, having first explained that he would not attend church in state or give the usual grand municipal banquet. Instead, he entertained members of the Council to dinner, without wine, and a larger number of guests at two soirées at the Grand Hotel. In Scarborough, Rowntree was a Borough magistrate, a Harbour Commissioner and sat on the School Board.

In 1886, during Rowntree's mayoralty, Gladstone was defeated over home-rule for Ireland which precipitated a general election. In order to stand as Scarborough's Liberal home-rule candidate for Parliament, Joshua Rowntree resigned as Mayor, incurring a £50 penalty. He was successful in the general election of 3 July 1886, getting 2,122 votes ousting Sir George Sitwell (q.v.), the sitting member, who got 2,020. In fact, Scarborough was one of only two Liberal gains in that election. The Conservatives formed a coalition with the Unionist Liberals forming an anti -home-rule administration. Rowntree remained member for Scarborough until 1892 when Sitwell re-took the seat. Rowntree was a staunch promoter of women's rights, amongst other things helping Florence Balgarnie, daughter of the local Congregational minister, to get elected to the first School Board in 1870 and another lady to be elected to the Board of Guardians in 1872.

Joshua Rowntree married Isabella Tindall, the eldest daughter of Robert Tindall (q.v.) in September 1880, away from Scarborough at the Friends' Meeting House in Ilkley. The Tindalls were Quaker ship owners who had been disowned by the Friends when, on the demand of their crews, they had armed their vessels against pirates. They were also Tories and the marriage away from Scarborough was said to save any embarrassment. Nonetheless, Joshua and Isabella returned to the Town to live in *Rawdon Villas*. Their only son Maurice was born in 1882. After being unsuccessful in the general election of 1892 Rowntree spent time travelling, visiting, amongst other places, Palestine in 1898, and Australia, New Zealand, and the United States in 1902-1903.

During the Boer War, Joshua Rowntree looked for ways to promote conciliation and peace. He organised a pro-peace meeting in Scarborough in March 1900 to be addressed by S. Cronwright Schreiner (1863-1936) a British subject from South Africa who was on a lecture tour in England. This resulted in mob violence against the Rowntree families and their properties, needing the local

Damage to John Rowntree's shop

militia to disperse the rioters. Between December 1900 and April 1901, Joshua Rowntree, his wife and nephew Harold T. Ellis (1875-1930), visited South Africa to investigate possible Quaker relief work, particularly in the concentration camps. Amongst the contacts they made there was a young Indian barrister, Mr Gandhi, who told them of the demoralising conditions to which all Asian people were subjected.

In 1912, Joshua Rowntree and his son rented *Worfolk*, a cottage near Staintondale owned by the Quakers. Joshua spent more and more time there until 1914, when, after a spell in a nursing home, he moved to *Wrea Head*, Scalby, where Maria Ellis, his widowed sister, lived. Joshua Rowntree died there in his sleep on 9 February 1915. He was survived by his widow and their only son Maurice Lotherington Rowntree.

Further reading
Scarborough Mercury 4 November 1892 (Address by Rowntree to Scarborough Women's Liberal Union)
Scarborough Pictorial 22 October 1913 (Biography)
Scarborough Mercury 12 February 1915 (Obituary)
Oxford Dictionary of National Biography
Binns, Jack, Heroes, Rogues and Eccentrics, A Biographical Journey Through Scarborough's Past, Blackthorn Press, 2002 pgs 200-208 (biography)
Binns, Jack, The History of Scarborough, North Yorkshire, Blackthorn Press, 2003 pgs 225-226 (Schreiner riots)
Robson S.E. Joshua Rowntree, George Allen & Unwin, London 1916 (Biography)
Rowntree, Arthur (ed.), The History of Scarborough, J. M. Dent, London 1931 pgs 307-398 (Schreiner riots)
Who's Who – Yorkshire, 1912, Westminster Publishing Co. Ltd London

SITWELL, Sir George Reresby, Bart.
1860 (London) - 1943 (Locarno, Switzerland)
Scarborough MP (Con.) 1885-1886 & 1892-1895

George Reresby Sitwell was born in Mayfair, London, on 27 January 1860. He was the only son of Sir Sitwell Reresby Sitwell, third baronet (1820-1862) and his wife Louisa Lucy, the daughter of Colonel the Hon. Henry Hely-Hutchinson. George's father died in 1862 and he became the fourth baronet at the age of two years. He was educated at Dr Chittenden's school, in Hoddesdon, Herts. followed by Eton College. He entered Christ Church College, Oxford in 1879 but left without taking his degree. While a student, it is reputed that he gained some notoriety by his *physical capture of a 'spirit' at a spiritualist headquarters in London.* While at Oxford he rowed, played cricket and boxed. During the vacations he travelled in Europe and on one occasion attended the coronation of the Tsar.

Sir George Sitwell entered politics at the age of 24. On 5 May 1884, he was accepted by the Conservatives of Scarborough as their candidate for the next Parliamentary election which was expected in 1885. However, in November of 1884, there were two Parliamentary by-elections fought in Scarborough within one month. The first was caused by the elevation of J. G. Dodson MP (q.v.) to the House of Lords on 23 October and the second when W. S. Caine MP (q.v.) accepted the post of Civil Lord of the Admiralty on 19 November which required him to seek re-election. Sitwell fought both by-elections and was unsuccessful in both. In the by-election of 3 November, Lieutenant-Colonel Steble (q.v.) was elected and in the by-election of 26 November, Caine was re-elected. In 1884, Scarborough's Parliamentary representation was reduced to one member and the franchise extended so that the majority of adult males had the vote. Sitwell stood in the general election the following year against the Liberal, John Glover and was successful. Although the Liberals won most seats in Parliament, they did not have an overall majority and the balance of power was held by the Irish Nationalists. This exacerbated divisions in the Liberal Party over home rule and a further general election was called the next year in July 1886. In this election, Sitwell lost to Joshua Rowntree (q.v.). In 1889, Sitwell bought a controlling interest in the *Scarborough Post* which became the organ of the local Conservative Party and in the general election of 1892 he won back the seat from Rowntree. George Sitwell then represented Scarborough until 1895 during which Parliament, as a confirmed Unionist, he voted against both of Mr Gladstone's Home Rule Bills. In 1895, he was defeated in Scarborough by J. Compton Rickett (q.v.) and again by Rickett in 1900. Thereafter, Sitwell did not stand again for Parliament and in 1908 he defected to the Liberal Party.

Sir George Sitwell's family seat was Renishaw Hall in Derbyshire and his Scarborough residence was *Woodend* in the Crescent. A keen antiquarian, he worked on inherited family papers writing *The First Whig*, a biography

31

of his ancestor, William Sacheverell and other related works. In 1900, he published *Letters of the Sitwells and Sacheverells*. His collection of books and papers were said to have filled seven sitting-rooms at Renishaw Hall.

Sitwell was a Captain of the Yorkshire Dragoons and Lieutenant-Colonel commanding the 2nd Volunteer Battalion P.W.O. Yorkshire Regiment. On the disbandment of the battalion, he retired with the rank of Colonel. In the First World War, Sir George was unfit for military service but farmed over 2,000 acres, producing large quantities of wheat and potatoes. Sir George was a Justice of the Peace both for Derbyshire and for Scarborough and he held the titles of Lord of the Manors of Eckington (Derbyshire), Whiston (Yorkshire) and Long Eckington (Warwickshire). He was founder of the Yorkshire Lawn Tennis Club in 1884.

On 23 November 1886, Sir George Sitwell married Lady Ida Emily Augusta Denison, daughter of William Henry Forester Denison (q.v.). They had three children, Edith (1887-1864), Osbert (1892-1969) and Sacheverell (1897-1988), all of whom followed prominent literary careers.

Sir George Sitwell had travelled extensively in Italy in his study of garden design and in 1909 purchased the *Castello di Montegufoni*, near Florence, a ruin inhabited by local peasants. Over the next three decades, he restored it to its original design and in 1925 took up permanent residence there. He wrote to both the Archbishop of Canterbury and the Chancellor of the Exchequer to explain that British taxes had forced him to settle in Italy. His wife died in 1937 but Sir George remained in Italy beyond the outbreak of the Second World War. However, in 1942, he moved to Switzerland where he died the following year at the *Villa Fontanelle*, Porto Ronco, Locarno on 9 July 1943.

Sir George was succeeded in the baronetcy by his elder son Osbert Sitwell.

Further reading
Scarborough Mercury 16 July 1943 (Obituary)
Oxford Dictionary of National Biography
Blakey, J.W. (ed.) Some Scarborough Faces, Past and Present, Scarborough Gazette Printing & Publishing Co. 1901 pgs 14 - 20 (Biography)
Binns, Jack, Heroes, Rogues and Eccentrics, A Biographical Journey Through Scarborough's Past, Blackthorn Press, 2002 pgs 190-199 (Biography)
Pearson, John, Facades, Edith, Osbert and Sacheverell Sitwell, Macmillan, London, 1978
Sitwell, George Reresby, Tales of My Native Village, O U Press, 1923

Sitwell, Osbert, Tales My Father Taught Me, Hutchinson, London, 1963
Who's Who – Yorkshire, 1912, Westminster Publishing Co. Ltd London.

STEBLE, Richard Fell
1836 (Lancs.) - 1899 (Scarborough)
Scarborough MP (Liberal) 1884-1885
Mayor 1891-1892

(This entry is repeated in the section on Mayors)

Richard Fell Steble was born on 15 September 1835, the son of Rev. J. H. Steble BA of Cambridge, formerly of Whicham, Cumberland. Richard was educated at Rossall College near Fleetwood. He qualified as a solicitor in 1858 and went into practice in Liverpool. In August 1859, he joined the First Lancashire Rifle Volunteers and moved through the ranks becoming Lieutenant Colonel in 1867, a position he held until 1876.

In 1867, Richard Steble was elected a Conservative councillor for North Toxteth, Liverpool and served on the City Council for 14 years. He was Mayor of Liverpool in 1874 and in 1875. During his mayoralty, the Lord Mayor of London visited the City with other mayors. Steble made a gift to Liverpool of a large fountain which was centrally placed in Lime Street near St George's Hall, the Art Gallery and Museum. In recognition of this a street was named after him.

In 1881, Steble came to live in Scarborough and soon entered local public life. In 1884, the Right Hon. J. D. Dodson (q.v.), the MP for Scarborough, was elevated to the peerage. In spite of having been a Conservative councillor in Liverpool, Steble was invited to contest the seat for the Liberals in the by-election of November of that year. He was successful against the Tory candidate, Sir George Sitwell (q.v.). However, Steble did not seek re-election in 1885 because of indifferent health and Sitwell won the seat.

Although not a member of Scarborough Council, Richard Steble was invited to become Mayor of the Borough in 1887 but he declined because of a recent accident. However, when invited in 1891, he did accept. His mayoral year was one long round of hospitalities, rich and poor being feted. He and his wife entertained 700 aged poor at the Grand Hotel at Christmas and they held an *At Home* in the Hotel which was attended by 900 guests. The Stebles held a series of popular concerts in the circus in St Thomas Street and as many as 2,000 attended the last one after which they entertained all of the artistes. Scarborough's cabmen, railwaymen and bath-chair men, together with their wives and children, were all entertained by the Mayor and his wife. On arrival in Scarborough, Steble was a Justice of the Peace for Liverpool and he became a JP for Scarborough and also for the North Riding. He was one of founders of the Scalby and Newby Agricultural Society and was President in 1899.

Richard Fell Steble was twice married. In June 1864, he married Elizabeth, the second daughter of John Garratt of Holywath, Coniston. Elizabeth died in May 1880. Steble then married Lily, the widow of John Metcalf of Pirzett, near Kendall by whom he had one daughter. His stepdaughter, Miss Metcalf-Steble, married Lieutenant Stansfeld, the adjutant of the local volunteers.

Richard Fell Steble died on 8 October 1899 at his residence *Ramsdale Bank*, 5, Belmont Road, Scarborough. He had suffered with sciatica while spending the summer at his country residence *The Knoll*, Bowness-on-Windermere. At the end of September he had had an apoplectic seizure but with treatment by Scarborough doctors Everley Taylor and Godfrey, Steble made a recovery. However, he had a second seizure on Sunday 8 October which was immediately fatal.

Richard Fell Steble was buried in Scarborough cemetery after a funeral service in Christ Church which the Mayor, Henry Darley (q.v.) attended along with most of the Corporation. In 1901, Steble's widow presented a Röntgen (X) Ray Apparatus to Scarborough Hospital and Dispensary in her husband's memory. Steble had been President of the Hospital in 1888, seven years before the discovery of X-rays by Wilhelm Konrad von Röntgen.

Further reading
Scarborough Mercury 13 October 1899 (Obituary)
Bayliss A. & P. & Jackson A., Scarborough Hospital and Dispensary, The First Fifty Years 1852-1902, Scarborough 2006 (Steble's involvement with the hospital)

STYLE, Sir Thomas Charles, Bart.
1787 (Kent) - 1879 (Bath)
                                    Scarborough MP (Whig) 1837-1841

Thomas Charles Style was born in August 1787 in Kent and was educated at the Royal Naval Academy at Gosport. In 1813, he inherited the title of 8th Baronet on the death of his brother. Style was a Deputy Lieutenant and magistrate for the County of Donegal and in 1824 was High Sheriff.

Thomas Style's connection with Scarborough began in 1822 when he married Isabella, the daughter of Sir George Cayley (q.v.). Style's political life in Scarborough commenced in 1835, when he was involved in the creation of the *Scarborough Association for the Protection and Extension of Civil and Religious Liberty*. The Association's first annual meeting was in January 1836 and Style was the principal speaker. He was also associated with the foundation of the *Scarborough Operatives Society* which had the objective of achieving religious and civil rights for working men. In the 1837 general election, Style stood as a Whig against the Tory, Sir Frederick Trench (q.v.), running with fellow Whig, Sir John V. B. Johnstone (q.v.). Style and Trench were elected to the two available Scarborough seats but Style did not contest any later elections in the Town.

Sir Thomas Style died on 23 July 1879 at his home, 102, Sydney Place, Bath in his 82nd year. He was succeeded in the baronetcy by William M. Style Esq., the son of his cousin, Captain W. Style RN.

Further reading
Scarborough Gazette 24 July 1879 (Obituary)
Scarborough Pictorial 7 January 1914 (Biography)

TRENCH, Sir Frederick W.
c. 1777 - 1859 (Brighton)

Scarborough MP (Tory) 1835-1847

Frederick William Trench was the elder son of Michael Frederick Trench (1746-1836) of Ballynakill, Ireland and his wife Anne Helena, daughter and heir of Patrick Stewart of Killymoon, County Tyrone. Frederick Trench went to school in Drogheda and, in 1793, continued his education at Trinity College, Dublin and then at Trinity College, Cambridge matriculating in 1797. He initially joined Lincoln's Inn, but opted for a military career and was commissioned into the First Foot Guards in 1803.

Trench served throughout the French Wars on the Quartermaster-General's Staff in Sicily, in the Walcheren expedition of 1809 and in Cadiz in 1811. In 1813, he was Deputy Quartermaster-General to the

35

Expeditionary Force to the Netherlands with the rank of Lieutenant-Colonel. When the war ended in 1814 he went onto half-pay. He was created KCH (Knight Commander of Hanover) in 1832, promoted to Major General in 1837, to Lieutenant-General in 1847 and made a General in 1854.

Trench's Parliamentary career was interwoven with his military life and began when he was returned for St Michael, Cornwall in the 1806 general election. This seat was in the patronage of Sir Christopher Hawkins who sold this and other of his pocket seats to men pledged to William Grenville's short lived *Government of all the Talents* (1806-1807). Trench vacated this seat in 1807. In 1812, Lord Roden brought Trench into Parliament again, this time for Dundalk, on the death of the sitting member. However, because of Trench's support for Catholic emancipation and occasions when Trench voted against the administration, Roden dropped him at the general election in October of the same year. He entered Parliament again in 1819 as member for Cambridge which was a pocket borough controlled by the Duke of Rutland to whom Trench was related by marriage. Trench held this seat until 1832.

As a Tory, Frederick Trench had opposed the Reform Bill in all its stages, describing it as *uncalled for, rash and revolutionary*. In 1832, at the first general election after the Reform Act, the two sitting members for Scarborough, Sir Charles Manners Sutton and the Hon. Edmund Phipps, both Tories, refused to stand. Prior to Parliamentary reform, one of Scarborough's seats was controlled by The Duke of Rutland who put Trench forward as the Tory candidate. Trench's electioneering included bribes, often liquid, dinners and theatres and he was especially attentive to fishermen and sailors who were a significant part of the Town's electorate. Whig handbills circulating in the Town before the election, produced by Scarborough printer James Bye, claimed that Trench supported slavery, flogged his soldiers, and ill treated his Irish tenants. Trench lost to his two Whig opponents Sir John Johnstone (q.v.) and Sir George Cayley (q.v.). In spite of this, Peel named him Secretary to the Master-General of the Ordnance during his short-lived administration of 1834 to 1835. Trench successfully stood again for Scarborough in the ensuing general election of 1835, was re-elected in 1837 and again in 1841. He returned to the Ordnance during Peel's second ministry (1842-1846) and was Scarborough's MP until 1847, when he resigned.

Sir Frederick Trench took a strong interest in architecture, both in Parliament and elsewhere. In 1820, he proposed a scheme to connect Pall Mall and Charing Cross with Blackfriars Bridge by an embankment on the north side of the River Thames. Detailed drawings were prepared in 1825 and an influential committee formed to carry them out but the scheme was never realised because of cost. He was involved in a project to create a giant equestrian statue of the Duke of Wellington to stand opposite the Duke's London residence, *Apsley House*, which Wellington himself said was *the damnedest job from the beginning*. In 1883, the sculpture was removed to Aldershot. In Scarborough, Trench was said to have suggested the design for Henry Wyatt's Gothic Saloon at the Spa, which was built in 1839.

Sir Frederick William Trench never married and died on 6 December 1859 at 81, Marine Parade, Brighton. In his will, he left all his Irish property to the eldest of his four sisters.

Further reading
Scarborough Mercury 17 December 1859 (Obituary)
Scarborough Pictorial 26 November 1913 (Biography)
Oxford Dictionary of National Biography
Binns, Jack, The History of Scarborough, North Yorkshire, Blackthorn Press, 2003 pgs 156-158 (1832 election).
Whittaker, Meredith, The Book of Scarborough Spaw, Barracuda Books Ltd, 1984 pg 89 (Trench and Scarborough Spa)

YOUNG, George Frederick
1791 (London) - 1870 (Reigate)

Scarborough MP (Tory) 1851-1852

George Frederick Young, born in 1791 in London, was the second son of Vice-Admiral William Young (1761-1847) and his wife Ann, daughter of Robert Curling. William Young was a partner of Robert Curling in the shipbuilding firm of *Curling, Young & Co.* George Young was educated mainly at home, joined the family business and, by the 1820s, was the senior partner in the firm. This became one of the most prominent of London's shipping concerns. It specialised in building East Indiamen, passenger ships and gun-ships. It also acquired interests in whaling and in the colonial trade. George Young was a member of the Committee of Lloyd's Register from 1825 to 1867, the longest serving founder member. He was also Chairman of the General London Ship Owners' Society. By the 1840s his shipping connections and interest in colonial reform led him to join other Tory ship-owners in the colonisation of New Zealand. Young purchased land there and he was a leading director of the New Zealand Company. His son, William Curling Young, also went to New Zealand but died there soon after his arrival in 1842.

George Young, as a supporter of shipping interests, entered Parliament in 1832 as member for Tynemouth. He mostly took the Whig whip but was seen as an independent with liberal views. He was returned for Tynemouth unopposed in 1835 and won a narrow victory there in 1837. While an MP, he spoke frequently in the House and Charles Dickens described him as a *prodigious bore*. However, in 1838, Young was unseated on technical grounds and, because of increasing business activities, he did not enter Parliament again until 1851. During these years he was a vital force in opposing free-trade and thus lent towards the Tories. In May 1849, he had set up the National Association for the Protection of British Industry and Capital, becoming its Chairman. In July 1851, one of Scarborough's MPs, Earl Mulgrave (q.v.) was appointed Comptroller of the Household which necessitated him seeking re-election in the Town. Mulgrave returned to Scarborough to canvass in the ensuing by-election, his one problem being that he supported free-trade. George Young came to Scarborough, as a total stranger, also to contest the by-election, standing as a Tory and a protectionist. He chose not to canvas the electorate but simply to state his principles and belief in trade protection. There were riots in the Town on the day of the election. In spite of the longstanding connection between Mulgrave and his family with Scarborough, George Young defeated him with 314 votes to 281. Earl Mulgrave accepted his defeat with bad grace.

However, Young's success was short lived. After being member for Scarborough for just one year there was a general election in 1852 at a time when he was ill. He was unable to come to Scarborough to support his candidature which was proposed by his brother, John Young, who confirmed that George was still a firm protectionist. His opponents were two Liberals, Sir John Johnstone (q.v.) and Earl Mulgrave (q.v.). In the ensuing election Young was defeated, Johnstone gaining 423 votes, Mulgrave 388 and Young 313. After this defeat, Young seems to have faded into political obscurity. His shipbuilding business was declining, as was whaling, because of American competition. However, he maintained his maritime interests through his involvement with Lloyd's Register and with the General London Ship Owners' Society.

George Young was a philanthropist and social reformer. He was unusual in living near to his London shipyards and involved himself in local community issues. Shoreditch in East London had the worst mortality rate in the Capital with very bad living conditions. Young obtained 30,000 signatures on a petition to the Queen in support of the creation of a local public park proposed by the reformer William Farr. The Queen gave permission for the park to take her name, the money for the project coming from the sale of *York House* in London. George Young also supported the building of baths and washhouses in the poorest quarters of the Capital. He was Chairman of the House Committee of the London Hospital from 1842 to 1844, Chairman of Stepney Board of Guardians for many years and founder of the Limehouse Children's Establishment (1838-1873). He was a Justice of the Peace and Deputy Lieutenant for Middlesex.

In 1814, George Young married Mary, the youngest daughter of John Abbot, a brewer of Canterbury and they had eight children. The family left the Limehouse area of London in the late 1840s and eventually settled in Reigate, apparently in straitened circumstances. George Young died there on 23 February 1870 and was buried in the churchyard of Reigate Parish Church survived by his wife. Their eldest surviving son, Frederick Young (1817-1913), inherited his father's colonial interests and became a leading member of the Royal Colonial Institute. Another son, Sidney (1821-1915), had taken over the family firm and later became a merchant assessor for the Admiralty Division of the High Court.

Further reading
Yorkshire Gazette Saturday 26 July 1851 (1851 Scarborough election)
Scarborough Gazette 3 March 1870 (Obituary)
Scarborough Pictorial 19 November 1913 (Biography)
Oxford Dictionary of National Biography

Scarborough Corporation 1896
Mayor & Mayoress Marillier centre

SCARBOROUGH'S MAYORS
1836 to 1906

INTRODUCTION

Samuel Standidge Byron (q.v.), a Roman Catholic, was elected the first Mayor of Scarborough in 1836 after a major reform of the Town's local government of which he was a major protagonist. Prior to this date, Scarborough's local affairs were in the hands of an undemocratic and corrupt Corporation.

The Old Corporation had consisted of 44 members, comprising two bailiffs, two coroners, four chamberlains and a common council of 36 divided into three benches of twelve each. The members of the Corporation, rather than the householders of the Town, had always voted for Scarborough's two Members of Parliament. Furthermore, the townsfolk had no role in choosing the Corporation. Although there was an annual 'election', members of the Corporation chose their fellow members. This meant that any of the 44 members could secure their seat for life merely by shifting place each year and nominating each other.

Not only was the Old Corporation undemocratic, it was also corrupt in various ways. Many of the members of the Corporation did not live in Scarborough. Henry Byron (Samuel's father) lived in London, Thomas Duesbury in Beverley, Dr Nathanial Travis in Malton, George Taylor in Filey and Stephen Armitage in Van Dieman's Land (i.e. Australia). Christopher Coulsen, collector of Customs at Whitby, had been an absentee member for 30 years. There were also concerns about nepotism. Given the system whereby members chose other members, many seats fell into the hands of single families. For example, immediately before the Old Corporation was abolished in 1836, it included six members of the Woodall banking family, six members of the Fowler family and four members of the Travis family while other members were related to one another by marriage.

There was also evidence of maladministration. Much property in the care of the Corporation, such as the piers and the gaol, was in a poor state of repair. The return from rents on Corporation property was claimed to be poor and some of its land and other assets had been sold, often to individual members of the Corporation.

The Great Reform Act of 1832 had taken away from Scarborough Corporation the power to select their Member of Parliament and had replaced it with a electorate of men who occupied a house or shop with an annual value of £10. In Scarborough, in the first election after the Act, the voters had sent two liberal minded Whigs, Sir George Cayley (q.v.) and Sir J. V. B. Johnstone (q.v.) to Parliament. Samuel Byron was Cayley's election agent. The national Government now turned its mind to the reform of municipal corporations and commissioners were appointed to inquire into their affairs.

His Majesty's Commissioners, Fortunatus Dwarris and S. A. Rumball, were appointed to look into Scarborough's affairs. The process was akin to that in a court of law, with a counsel for the defence, which comprised a Town Hall Committee including John Woodall senior and the Town Clerk and a counsel for the prosecution which was led by Samuel Byron. Byron, a known reformer, had been appointed to the Corporation in 1829 in a manner reminiscent of its undemocratic nature. He had been approached by a friend, John Wharton, who wanted to marry Byron's sister-in-law and offered him a nomination for a vacancy on the Corporation which was at the disposal of Wharton's uncle. In spite of violent opposition, Byron joined the Old Corporation in April 1830 and, not surprisingly, he was the only member seeking reform, although he had many allies in the Town. When the Commissioners left Scarborough, the Corporation believed that it had satisfactorily answered all of their questions and a petition was sent to the House of Lords, asking that the Town be exempted from municipal reform. However, in January 1834, the Commissioners published their report which was a damning review of the Town's governance.

Reform was thus inevitable. Under the Municipal Corporations Act, the Borough, which kept its original boundaries, was divided into two wards – a North and a South, each with nine seats on the new Council. There was an electorate of 549 rate-paying male adult residents and the first elections were held on 28 December 1835. The liberal reformers of the Town put up 19 candidates against the old Tories and took 17 out of the 18 seats, the only Tory elected being John Woodall. This result was mirrored across Yorkshire where all the Boroughs went to the Whig reformers, except in Ripon. Samuel Byron, who had prosecuted the Old Corporation before the Commissioners, came top of the poll in the North Ward. Six of new council members were elevated to be Aldermen and the six replacements chosen were also reformers including John Rowntree the Quaker grocer.

Not only did the reforms introduce a new more democratic system of local government in Scarborough but also a modernised administration including monthly meetings with public reports and the appointment of a Town Clerk and a Treasurer who were not members of the Council. Other posts such as police chief, coroner and harbour master were soon filled by competent men.

Samuel Standidge Byron was elected the first mayor of the Borough in January 1836 a post he held until November of that year when he was required to resign in rotation. Thereafter Scarborough's mayors were elected for an annual period from November each year.

In 1884, as a result of the growth of Scarborough, Commissioners from the Privy Council visited the Town to review its wards. They divided the Town into six new wards, - North, North-West, West, South, East and Central, each returning three councillors.

A further change to the system of local government came with the Local Government Act 1888 which created county councils across the country. As a result, Scarborough returned six councillors to the North Riding County Council, one from each of the Town's wards.

Further reading
The Burgess, published by Ainsworth, Scarborough, 1836
A Report of the Inquiry into the State of the Corporation of Scarborough (27th & 28th November 1833) before Fortunatus Dwarris and S. A. Rumball esq.s, Hull, 1834
Blakey, J.W. (ed.) Some Scarborough Faces, Past and Present, Scarborough Gazette Printing & Publishing Co. 1901 pgs 244-251 (Scarborough Corporation)
Binns, Jack, The History of Scarborough, North Yorkshire, Blackthorn Press, 2003 Chapter 12

CHRONOLOGICAL LIST
of
SCARBOROUGH MAYORS
1836 – 1906

1836	Councillor Samuel Standidge Byron
1836-37	Alderman William Harland MD
1837-38	Councillor John Hesp
1838-39	Alderman Thomas Weddell
1839-40	Councillor Thomas Purnell
1840-41	Alderman Robert Tindall
1841-42	Alderman Robert Tindall
1842-43	Councillor William Harland
1843-44	Alderman Robert Tindall
1844-45	Councillor Thomas Weddell
1845-46	Councillor Thomas Purnell
1846-47	Alderman Robert Tindall
1847-48	Councillor John Hesp
1848-49	Councillor William Harland MD
1849-50	Alderman Robert Tindall
1850-51	Councillor Edward Hopper Hebden
1851-52	Councillor John Woodall
1852-53	Councillor John Hesp
1853-54	Councillor John Fairgray Sharpin
1854-55	Alderman George Willis
1855-56	Alderman William Holden
1856-57	Alderman John Wheldon
1857-58	Councillor Henry Spurr
1858-59	Councillor Hodgson Smith
1859-60	Councillor John Barry
1860-61	Councillor Richard Cross MD
1861-62	Alderman Godfrey Knight
1862-63	Alderman Godfrey Knight
1863-64	Councillor John Haigh
1864-65	Councillor Ambrose Gibson
1865-66	Councillor Ambrose Gibson
1866-67	Councillor Robert Champley
1867-68	Councillor Robert Champley
1868-69	Councillor John Woodall Woodall
1869-70	Councillor Robert Forster

1870-71	Councillor William Foster Rooke MD
1871-72	Councillor William Foster Rooke MD
1872-73	Councillor Joseph Williamson
1873-74	Councillor George White
1874-75	Alderman George Porrett
1875-76	Councillor John Hart
1876-77	Councillor Benjamin Fowler
1877-78	Councillor Benjamin Smith
1878-79	Councillor William Charles Land
1879-80	Councillor Samuel North Smith
1880-81	Councillor Thomas Whittaker
1881-82	Alderman John Woodall Woodall
1882-83	Councillor William Barry
1883-84	Councillor Pantland Hick jun.
1884-85	Alderman Robert Forster
1885-86	Councillor Joshua Rowntree
1886-87	Alderman John Woodall Woodall
1887-88	Leasowe Walker Esq.
1888-89	Councillor James Hutton
1889-90	Councillor James Hutton
1890-91	Councillor Henry Darley
1891-92	Lieut. Colonel Richard Fell Steble
1892-93	John Dale Esq.
1893-94	George Lord Beeforth Esq.
1894-95	Alderman Valentine Fowler
1895-96	Alderman Henry Merry Cross
1896-97	Councillor Robert Aspland Marillier
1897-98	Councillor James Pirie
1898-99	Councillor Henry Darley
1899-1900	Councillor Henry Darley
1900-01	Councillor Henry Darley
1901-02	Councillor Joseph Sinfield
1902-03	William Morgan Esq.
1903-04	Councillor William Morgan
1904-05	Councillor William Morgan
1905-06	Alderman William Hastings Fowler
1906-07	Councillor John Watson Rowntree

SCARBOROUGH'S MAYORS
1836 to 1906

THE DICTIONARY

BARRY, John
1803 (Scarborough) - 1866 (Scarborough)

Mayor 1859-1860

John Barry was born in 1803, the son of William Barry of Sledmere and Ann, neé Cooper and was baptised at St Mary's Parish Church, Scarborough on 25 September. John Barry became a stonemason, architect, brick-maker and building contractor in Scarborough and in 1828 won a contract from the Cliff Bridge Company for work at Scarborough Spa. He continued working there on various projects for the next 30 years including building Henry Wyatt's *Gothic Saloon* (1839). As an architect Barry's work included Newborough Bar (1831 demolished 1848), St Stephen's Church at Snainton near Scarborough (1835), Wilson's Mariners' Homes in Castle Road, Scarborough (1836) and parts of Filey Crescent (1840-53). John Barry's brick and stoneware factory in Barry's Lane off Seamer Road was producing 7-10 million bricks a year in the 1860s, drawing complaints of pollution from nearby neighbours.

Further afield, Barry gained two large contracts in Scotland. In the 1840s he was working in Arbroath where he had the contract to build a new harbour and in Leith he was the contractor for the Victoria Dock, 1847-1852, employing his son William (q.v.) as superintendent.

John Barry returned to Scarborough in the mid-1850s and was elected a councillor for the North Ward. In 1859, he was made Mayor for the period 1859 to 1860.

John Barry was married twice. With his first wife, Mary Ann, he had three sons. William, born 1828, and John born 1833, both became builders and architects in Scarborough, William (q.v.) becoming Mayor for the period 1882 to 1883. Their third son, Thomas, born 1834, was also a builder and after working in Allahabad, for the East India Railway, settled in York. John Barry's wife, Mary Ann, died in June 1853 at the age of 47. In June 1855 John Barry married Martha Thornton, daughter of Jeremiah Thornton of Birks Hall, Bradford.

South Cliff Congregational Church (today St Andrew's Church), which was opened in 1865, was John Barry's last major building contract. He died the next year on 26 November 1866 and was buried in Scarborough Cemetery. A Baptist, John Barry was said in a local newspaper obituary to have been *admired as one of the best employers* in Scarborough.

Further reading
Bayliss A & P, Architects and Civil Engineers of Nineteenth Century Scarborough, A Biographical Dictionary, Scarborough 2001(Biography and his works)

BARRY, William
1828 (Scarborough) - 1898 (Scarborough)

Mayor 1882-1883

William Barry was the eldest son of Scarborough building contractor John Barry (q.v.), who was Mayor for the period 1859 to 1860, and like his father became a builder and architect. As a young boy William worked with Sir Martin Peto building railways in Norfolk and Suffolk. In the late 1840s he went to Scotland where he supervised his father's contract to build the Victoria Dock at Leith.

William returned to Scarborough and was appointed surveyor to the Scarborough Improvement Commissioners after the death of John Irvin in 1853. As a builder and architect he was responsible for the Dispensary in Elder Street (1858), the Cottage Hospital, Spring Hill Road (1870), Haddo Terrace, Aberdeen Walk, Albemarle Crescent and the Royal Crescent, where he built his own house - *Royal Crescent Lodge*. William Barry was a partner in his father's brick, tile and terracotta manufacturing business in Barry's Lane off Seamer Road. He continued to run the business after his father's death but later leased it out.

Although Barry was a prominent member of the Albemarle Baptist Church having previously belonged to the Ebenezer Chapel, he was elected an unsectarian member of the School Board from 1874 - 1880. He was first elected as a Liberal councillor for the South Ward in 1877 and in 1878 was made a Borough Magistrate. Barry was made Mayor for the period 1882 to 1883. During his mayoralty, Scarborough Corporation approached the eminent civil engineer, Sir John Coode to give his opinion on the feasibility of building a road under Castle Cliff to join the north and south bays, for which he prepared a series of reports from 1882 to 1889. Royal Albert Drive was opened in 1890 and Marine Drive in 1908. In 1885, Barry gave land for the enlargement of the Rotunda Museum. In 1890, he was appointed a magistrate for the North Riding. He was Chairman of the Burial Board and took great interest in the lay out of the cemetery. He was a trustee of the Municipal Charities and also of the Cottage Hospital. He was on the Committee of Scarborough Hospital and Dispensary and was President in 1883. He was a Harbour Commissioner and a member of the Cliff Bridge Company, which ran Scarborough Spa.

In 1849, William Barry married Selina Grayburn, the youngest daughter of William Richardson of Hunmanby in the Parish Church there. At the time Barry was still working in Leith where their first son, Frederick William, was born March 1851. He became a Doctor of Medicine, Doctor of Science and a Barrister at Law but died suddenly at the early age of 46 in October 1897 while on official duties in Birmingham. Their second son, Charles was born in Scarborough in 1863 and became Vicar of Clifford, Boston Spa.

William Barry's wife Selina died three months after the sudden death of their son Frederick. Broken by these two deaths William died suddenly at his home on 7 April 1898.

Further reading
Scarborough Gazette 7 April 1898 (Obituary)
Bayliss A & P, Architects and Civil Engineers of Nineteenth Century Scarborough, A Biographical Dictionary, Scarborough 2001(Biography and works)
Bayliss A & P and Jackson, Alan, Scarborough Hospital and Dispensary, the First Fifty Years, 1852-1902, Scarborough 2006 (Building of Dispensary)

BEEFORTH, George Lord
1823 (Scarborough) - 1924 (Scarborough)

Mayor 1893-1894

George Lord Beeforth (Lord was a family name) was born on Easter Sunday 1823, the son of Captain George Beeforth and his wife Susannah. Beeforth's father had retired from the merchant navy where he had been employed during the Peninsular War and had set up as a Grocer in Newborough Street, Scarborough. He died in 1833, leaving a widow and six children, with ages ranging from one to 17 years, George, aged 10, being the only boy. A distant cousin, Rev. Joseph Skelton, paid for his education at Scarborough Grammar School.

George Beeforth was then apprenticed to a Scarborough bookseller. When he completed his articles, he set up his own business in St Nicholas Street with capital provided by Rev. Skelton, who by now had the living of both Wykeham and Wold Newton Churches. Beeforth described his business as printer, bookseller, stationer, print and music seller, bookbinder and newspaper agent and he included an art gallery of circulating paintings of the day. The business prospered and in 1864 Beeforth sold it and together with James Liddle Fairless, a Newcastle printer and publisher, they set up an art gallery in London. Here Beeforth and Fairless  displayed and sold mainly the work of the French artist Gustave Doré. In 1889, when Beeforth was 66, he sold the London gallery and returned to Scarborough. He invested much of his money in building the terrace of houses from the Prince of Wales Terrace to, but excluding, Red Court on Scarborough's Esplanade. The development included Beeforth's own house, *Belvedere*.

Before moving to London, Beeforth had been a councillor for the South Ward from 1866 to 1869. On his return to Scarborough in 1889 he took no formal part in local politics although in that year he was appointed a magistrate for the North Riding. In 1893, although not a councillor, he was asked if he would put himself forward to be Mayor to which he agreed and he was duly elected. After his 1893/94 tenure he was twice asked to consider being elected again but on both occasions refused.

In 1854, George Lord Beeforth married Helen Crawford (1813-1894), the daughter of a Scarborough jeweller. His wife had previously taught music and languages and her knowledge of French had helped Beeforth in his negotiations with Gustave Doré. Their only son, Henry Alicis, born 1856, died in Italy in March 1893 just before Beeforth's term as mayor while his wife Helen died during his term of office in July 1894. Beeforth continued to live in Scarborough and pursued many artistic and intellectual interests.

George Lord Beeforth died on 12 April 1924 at the age of 101 and is buried in the family grave at Scalby four miles North of Scarborough.

Further reading

Scarborough Post 24 December 1897 (Presentation of his portrait to the Town)
Scarborough Pictorial 29 October 1913 (Biographical article)
Scarborough Mercury 6 April 1923 (His centenary celebrations)
Scarborough Mercury 17 April 1924 (Obituary)
Bayliss A & P, George Lord Beeforth, 1823-1924, Grand Old Man of Scarborough, Transactions of Scarborough Archaeological and Historical Society, No.36, 2000, pgs 7-27 (Biography)
Blakey, J.W. (ed.) Some Scarborough Faces, Past and Present, Scarborough Gazette Printing & Publishing Co. 1901 pgs 8-13 (Biography)

BYRON, Samuel Standidge
1800 (Scarborough) - 1879 (Snainton)

Mayor 1836

Samuel Standidge Byron was born in Scarborough in 1800, the son of Henry Byron (1774-1854), a member of the Old Corporation of Scarborough. Samuel's mother Jane was the daughter of John Thornton of Hull and granddaughter of Sir Samuel Standidge, a famous Mayor of Hull. Samuel Byron was educated St Peter's School, York, boarding with the Rev. Isaac Grayson. At about the age of 19, Byron went into the shipping business, working at various times in London, Hull and Archangel. In his early 20s he bought a West India ship and visited South America, Madeira, the Canaries and Le Havre. When his ship lay in Scarborough harbour for three days, it was reported that 4,000 visitors came to see it.

In the late 1820s, Samuel Byron returned to Scarborough and in 1829 was elected a Piers and Harbours Commissioner. In this year, a friend, John Wharton, wanted to marry Byron's sister-in-law and offered him a nomination for a vacancy on the Old Corporation which was at the disposal of Wharton's uncle. There was violent opposition to Byron, a known reformer, joining the Corporation. However, in April 1830 he became a member and continued to seek reform of the Old Corporation, citing absenteeism and nepotism, the poor state of the piers, gaols and other property in the care of the Corporation (see Introduction for details). In fact, Byron's father who lived in London and had been a bailiff, 1815-16, was one of the absentee members young Byron objected to.

Byron was very active in Yorkshire Whig politics. He was Chairman of Sir George Cayley's (q.v.) Committee when he and Sir J. V. B. Johnstone (q.v.) were returned as MPs for Scarborough in 1832 and at the same time

Chairman of a similar Committee in Pickering Lythe East for the candidature of E. S. Cayley as MP for the North Riding.

Byron was appointed leader of the Whigs in their presentation to the Parliamentary Commissioners arguing for reform of Scarborough's local governance (see Introduction). Once the Municipal Corporations Act had been approved by Parliament, elections were held in Scarborough on 28 December 1835 and the Liberals took 17 of the 18 seats on the reformed Council. Byron topped the poll in the North Ward and the new council elected him as the first mayor of the reformed Borough, a post he held until November 1836 when he had to retire by rotation. In the same year he was appointed a Justice of the Peace for the Borough, three years later, for the North Riding and in 1856 for the East Riding. When, in 1855, it was agreed that a Burial Board should be formed in Scarborough under the provisions of the Burial Grounds Act, Samuel Byron, a Roman Catholic, was one of its earliest members and represented their interests.

In 1824, Samuel Byron married Sophia, daughter of Captain Lowe of the Royal Irish Fencibles but she died after a few months. The following year he married Elizabeth, daughter of Thomas Candler of the *Low Hall*, West Ayton by whom he had a son and two daughters. Their son, Thomas, born 1836, like his father was a County Magistrate and land owner. One of their daughters, Agnes, married John Austin of Castleford, later Sir John Austin, 1st Baronet.

Byron's wife, Elizabeth, died in 1859 at their home in Westfield Terrace, Scarborough. About 1862, Samuel Byron withdrew from public life and lived abroad for many years, mainly in Belgium. He later returned to Yorkshire to live at West Ayton but died at his son Thomas's home, *Snainton Ings House*, Snainton on 30 January 1879.

Further reading
Scarborough Gazette 6 February 1879 (Obituary)
Binns, Jack, The History of Scarborough, North Yorkshire, Blackthorn Press, 2003 Chapter 12 (Politics).
Rowntree, Arthur (ed.), The History of Scarborough, J. M. Dent, London 1931 pgs 303-305 (Biography)

CHAMPLEY, Robert
1830 (Scarborough) -1895 (Scarborough)
Mayor 1866-1867 & 1867-1868

Robert Champley was born in Scarborough in 1830, the son of John Champley (1792-1864), a chemist of Newborough. Robert was initially educated at Scarborough Grammar School and afterwards at St Peter's School, York. He was articled to the engineer, Robert Stephenson and then studied architecture but followed neither profession. He later studied zoology under Schlegel in Leyden and Milne Edwards in Paris. Returning to Scarborough he lived the life of a gentleman of independent means and was a keen collector of natural history objects. It was reported that he had a Great Auk and egg which was *known throughout Europe*. Although a supporter of Scarborough Philosophical Society, he  was very conservative and his influence over the institution almost stopped its growth.

Robert Champley was first elected to the Town Council in 1863 for the North Ward and was again returned in 1866 and 1869. During this time he was made Mayor of the Borough in 1866 for the period 1866 to 1867 and again for the period 1867 to 1868. Although Champley attended Council meetings, it was reported that he took little part in the management of the Town. In 1864, Robert Champley was appointed a Justice of the Peace for Scarborough and in 1870 he was elected Alderman. In 1875, he became a Justice of the Peace and in 1890 was appointed Deputy Lieutenant, both for the North Riding. At various times he was a Harbour Commissioner, a Land and Income Tax Commissioner, a Trustee of the Municipal Charities and Vice-President of the Savings Bank. Although he contested a seat on the School Board three times, he did not succeed.

Champley donated a font to the Parish Church which was uncovered on Easter Day, 4 April 1869, for the baptism of his daughter Constance. Some re-arrangement of the church was necessary for the positioning of the font and it was described in the Scarborough Mercury as ...*Early English*... and ... *massive and handsome*... The bowl was of Portland stone and the whole was designed by George Bodley, the architect of St Martin's-on-the-Hill,

Scarborough and made by *Messrs Field & Co.* of Westminster. Champley also presented plate to Scarborough Corporation.

Robert Champley married Sarah Elizabeth Mary, daughter of Richard Barfell Phipson of Warwickshire in February 1866 and they had three daughters. Mrs Champley died in 1892.

Robert Champley died suddenly on 29 January 1895, in the street. At the time he was discussing with the undertaker, Mr Tonks, funeral arrangements for his close friend Dr Samuel Fitch. Champley was buried at All Saints Church, Thornton Dale, where he owned much property inherited from his father.

Further reading
Scarborough Mercury 1 February 1895 (Obituary)
Blakey, J.W. (ed.) Some Scarborough Faces, Past and Present, Scarborough Gazette Printing & Publishing Co. 1901 pgs 84 - 86 (Biography)

CROSS, Henry Merry
1830 (Burniston, nr Scarborough) - 1910 (Scarborough)
Mayor 1895-1896

Henry Merry Cross was born in 1830 at Burniston, the son of Robert Merry Cross, a gardener and seedsman of Scalby, near Scarborough. By the age of 20, Henry was also working as a gardener in Scalby. After marrying in 1857, Henry worked in London for four years before returning to Scalby in the early 1860s. In 1864, he was elected to the post of local Poor Law Guardian but later obtained the more  remunerative post of Assistant Poor Law Overseer for the Scarborough Union and he moved to Claremont Crescent in the Town. One responsibility of his new post was the compilation of the Burgess Roll for Scarborough, the annual list of those eligible to vote. Omissions in the list in 1874 caused public criticism of Cross with hints of political bias on his part but he robustly and successfully defended himself against such accusations.

Henry Merry Cross was elected a member of the first Scarborough School Board in

1871, a position he held for 18 years. He was a Liberal in politics and in 1883, out of 300 applicants, he was appointed secretary of the North Riding Liberal Association. In 1889, he was elected to the Town Council for the West Ward and was made Mayor of the Borough for the period 1895 to 1896.

Amongst his public roles, Cross was one of the originators of the Scalby Water Company of which he was a director. He instigated a petition to the Duchy of Lancaster for an extension to the Scalby graveyard resulting in an acre of land being donated. For sometime he was a highways surveyor and was a strong advocate of building the Scarborough-Whitby railway. He was also connected with Scarborough Amicable Society, an educational charity, and Scarborough Mechanics' Institute. He was one of the founders of the Scalby Temperance Movement, about 1854, and was one of four co-purchasers of premises opposite the *Nag's Head* public house there which were converted for use for meetings. Later, this property was demolished and a Temperance Hall, designed by *Messrs Stark & Rowntree* of Glasgow was erected in 1894.

In 1857, Henry Merry Cross married Elizabeth, the daughter of John Stonehouse, a Scalby farmer. They had at least five children but one son, Erasmus Henry, died at the early age of 19 in 1880.

Henry Merry Cross died on 29 November 1910, aged 80 and was buried in Scalby churchyard.

Further reading
Blakey, J.W. (ed.) Some Scarborough Faces, Past and Present, Scarborough Gazette Printing & Publishing Co. 1901 pgs 118-121 (Biography)
Whitworth, Alan, Villages Tales, the Story of Scalby and Its Residents. Alan Sutton Publishing, 1993 (Scalby and the Temperance Movement)

CROSS, Richard
1818 (Heslerton) - 1882 (Scarborough)

Mayor 1860-1861

Richard Cross was the second son of David Cross, a Heslerton farmer. Richard served an apprenticeship with Mr R. Rennison, a Sherburn surgeon, before studying medicine at Guy's Hospital, London. He gained his Licentiate of the Society of Apothecaries (LSA) in 1839 and his Membership of the Royal College of Surgeons (MRCS) in 1840 and returned to Scarborough to set up in medical practice. In 1852, he obtained his doctorate (MD) from St Andrew's University. In 1881, he was elected a Fellow of the Royal College of Surgeons (FRCS).

During his years as surgeon in Scarborough, Richard Cross was at various times in partnership with Thomas Weddell (q.v.), Henry Wright and later with his own son, Thomas Brown Cross. Richard Cross held many appointments in his medical capacity including being surgeon to the Royal Northern Sea-bathing Infirmary and surgeon to the East and North Riding Yorks Artillery Volunteers. For 36 years, he was Medical Officer to the Ancient Order of the Foresters Friendly Society. He was also on the Committee of the Cliff Bridge Company which managed Scarborough Spa.

Richard Cross was first elected to the Town Council in 1849 as a representative for the North Ward. He was re-elected at each election until 1862. In 1860, he was made Mayor of the Borough for the period 1860 to 1861. During his mayoralty the foundation stone of the Westborough Wesleyan Chapel was laid and the Jubilee Primitive Methodist Chapel in Aberdeen Walk was opened. Also during his mayoral year, new buildings for the Lancasterian Schools were begun. In January 1861, Cross was appointed the first Honorary Surgeon to the newly formed Scarborough Artillery Volunteer Corps. In 1862, he was elected an Alderman and in 1866 a Borough Magistrate. He was a Trustee of the Municipal Charities and finally retired from the Town Council in 1874. Richard Cross was a Methodist and was a Trustee of the Queen Street Wesleyan Chapel.

In 1845, he married Rachel Brown, daughter of George Brown, a Hull ship-owner, at St Mary's, Hull. They had three sons, Rev. George F. B. Cross became Vicar of All Saints, Small Heath, Birmingham, Richard N. Cross became an engineer and Thomas Brown Cross qualified as a doctor and became a partner in his father's practice which he continued after Richard's death.

Richard Cross died on 18 November 1882, after an amputation of his leg by the leading Leeds surgeon, Mr Jessop. Dr Cross had been in great pain for two years from a swollen thigh following a series of falls. He had previously consulted Mr Jessop who, on this occasion, was visiting Scarborough for a meeting of the British Medical Association and decided to amputate. There was great sadness across the town at Cross's death. His funeral, both civic and military, was attended all along the route of the cortege and at the cemetery by huge crowds and was said *to be one of the most numerously attended funerals* that had ever taken place in Scarborough. The procession was headed by the police, the band of the Artillery Volunteers and the Firing Party of the Artillery Volunteers. The

Mayor and Corporation in the procession were in their formal robes. The funeral services were conducted by Rev. S. Whitehead, Wesleyan Minister. Richard Cross's wife continued to live in the family home, *Carlton House*, South Cliff until her death in 1906, aged 91.

Further reading
Scarborough Gazette 23 November 1882 (Obituary)
Scarborough Mercury 24 November 1882 (Obituary)
Bayliss, A & P, The Medical Profession in Scarborough, 1700 to 1899, Scarborough 2005 (Biography)

DALE, John
1832 (Lancaster) - 1903 (Scarborough)

Mayor 1892-1893

John Dale was born in Lancaster on 22 May 1832, the son of Francis and Jane Dale. John was educated in Lancaster and began his career as a partner in *Messrs Hodgson & Dale,* agents of London and York. He later joined *Messrs Simon & Lightly* which soon became *Messrs Simon & Dale*. Most of the firm's business was conducted by Dale until 1882, when he was ordered to retire for health reasons. At the time of his retirement, he was the sole agent for *Moët and Chandon* champagne in Great Britain and the Colonies.

John Dale had been a frequent visitor to Scarborough and when he gave up his business he moved to the Town. He had a house, *Netherbank*, Filey Road, built for him in 1883, designed by the York architect, James Demaine and Dale then settled in the Town. In spite of his poor state of health, he immediately immersed himself in local charitable work. He was quoted to have *soon discovered an under-stratum of bottomless poverty* in Scarborough and he joined the Charity Organisation Society, becoming its Honorary Secretary in 1885. He set about improving the efficiency of the Society, having the premises enlarged and the record keeping improved. He was also associated with the Society for the Prevention of Cruelty to Children and the Society for the Prevention of Cruelty to Animals.

John Dale played a major role in the erection of a new hospital in Scarborough. In March 1891, as President-elect of Scarborough Hospital and Dispensary (he was President 1891-1893), he proposed a site for a new building and a scheme for financing it which was accepted by the Hospital Board. The new Hospital was opened in Friars Entry in 1893 and served Scarborough until 1936.

Although not a member of the Town Council, John Dale was approached in November 1892 to become Mayor for the period 1892-1893. It is said that he accepted only because of the help this would give to his hospital project. He was reported to have been no orator but an excellent organiser. During his mayoral year there were formal civic celebrations in Scarborough for the marriage of HRH the Duke of York and these were combined with the official opening of the new hospital by the Mayor. In the evening, the Mayor and Mayoress held an *At Home* for 800 guests at the Grand Hotel.

John Dale was a director of the Scarborough-Whitby Railway from 1887 becoming Chairman in 1892 on the death of Robert Forster (q.v.). At various times, Dale was a director of the Scarborough Electric Supply Company, President of Scarborough School of Art in 1893, a member of the Board of the Royal Northern Sea-bathing Infirmary, a Trustee of Scarborough Cottage Hospital and a Land and Income Tax Commissioner. In politics, he was a Conservative and had been appointed a Justice of the Peace for the North Riding in 1886.

In 1867, John Dale married, Lydia, the fourth daughter of Mr Wells Hood of York but they had no children. John Dale died at his house, *Netherbank*, on 3 October 1903, after a prolonged illness. His funeral was held on 6 October, at St Martin's-on-the-Hill Church, Scarborough with the Bishop of Hull, Archdeacon Charles Mackarness and Rev. E. M. Roberts officiating. John Dale was buried in Scarborough Cemetery.

Further reading
Scarborough Mercury 9 October 1903 (Obituary)
Bayliss A & P and Jackson, Alan, Scarborough Hospital and Dispensary, the First Fifty Years, 1852-1902, Scarborough 2006 (Building of the new hospital)
Blakey, J.W. (ed.) Some Scarborough Faces, Past and Present, Scarborough Gazette Printing & Publishing Co. 1901 pgs 2-7 (Biography)

DARLEY, Henry
1839 (Huttons Ambo) - 1904 (Scarborough)
Mayor 1890-1891, 1898-1899, 1899-1900 & 1900-1901

Henry Darley was born on 9 September 1839, the son of Henry Brewster Darley of Aldby Park, a member of a very old Yorkshire family. Henry junior became a Youth Officer in the 5th Dragoon Guards but in 1860, at the age of 21, he succeeded to the family estates on the sudden death of his father. Although he retired from the army he kept up an interest in military affairs and was Captain of a group of Yorkshire Yeomanry (Hussars). While living in *Ravine Villa*, Filey, Darley was also Captain of the East Riding Artillery Volunteers.

Unfortunately, Henry Darley became bent up with chronic rheumatism and retired to Scarborough in the 1880s where he began to take an interest in the affairs of the Town. An ardent Conservative, he was elected to the Town Council in November 1889 for the South Ward which he also represented on the County Council (1889 to 1901). Darley was made Mayor of the Borough for the year 1890 to 1891. The major event of this mayoralty was the visit of the Northern Squadron of 22 naval ships which anchored in the South Bay. Seven years later he was again made Mayor for the year 1898-99 and again for the following two years, 1899-1900 and 1900-1901. During his mayoralties he inaugurated a branch of the Patriotic Fund during the South African War, where his eldest son Henry Algernon, was serving and Scarborough raised £1,500. He also established the Warm Clothing Fund and a local Indian Famine Fund which raised £893. Darley was much involved with the ceremonies when, in August 1900, the Lord Mayor of London came to Scarborough, formally to open St Nicholas Gardens and the Belvedere Gardens.

Darley was a Justice of the Peace for the North Riding from 1884 and for the Borough from 1894. Also in 1894, he was elected to a seat on the Board of Guardians and remained a member until 1904 when he retired. He was a member of Scarborough School Board 1895-98, President of Scarborough Cricket Club for a time and was on the committee of the Cliff Bridge Company which managed Scarborough Spa.

58

In 1903, Henry Darley was awarded the Freedom of the Borough of Scarborough at the same time as Earl Feversham and Alderman W. C. Land (q.v.).

Henry Darley's first wife died within a year of their marriage. He then married Rosamund, the daughter of Sir George Cholmley and they had several children. Mrs Darley died after a long illness in 1894.

Henry Darley died on Christmas morning 1904 at his Scarborough home in the Crescent. He had been in failing health for some time. A memorial service was held in Christ Church, Scarborough by Archdeacon Mackarness and Rev. A. J. Shields. Darley's body taken by train to be buried on 28 December 1904 in the churchyard of Buttercrambe, near Aldby Park, where there was a large gathering of his tenants and local villagers. He was survived by his elder son, Henry Algernon C. Darley, who was in the Yorks Artillery and had served in the South African War.

In 1905, money was raised to install a patient hand-lift in Scarborough Hospital as a memorial to Captain Henry Darley who had been a supporter of that institution. The associated memorial plaque is now situated in the foyer of the present Town Hall.

Further reading
Scarborough Mercury 30 December 1904 (Obituary)
Scarborough Pictorial 11 March 1914 (Biography)
Blakey, J.W. (ed.) Some Scarborough Faces, Past and Present, Scarborough Gazette Printing & Publishing Co. 1901 pgs 92-94 (Biography)
Scott, W. Herbert, ed. W. T. Pike, North and East Ridings of Yorkshire Contemporary Biographies at the Opening of XX Century, Brighton 1903 (Biography)

FORSTER, Robert
1817 (Carlisle) - 1892 (Scarborough)

Mayor 1869-1870 & 1884-1885

Robert Forster was born in Carlisle in 1817. He came to Scarborough in 1846 as manager for Henry Hopkins, a grocer and tea dealer of 75, Newborough Street. The business had been founded in 1782 and Forster bought the business from Hopkins about 1849. By 1851 Forster was employing an assistant and an apprentice.

ESTABLISHED 1782.

ROBERT FORSTER,
(Successor to H. Hopkins,)

GROCER, TEA-DEALER, &c., 75, Newbro' Street, Scarbro'.

Yorkshire Hams and Tongues. Agent for Carr's Fancy Biscuits. Rich and delicious Sauces, Pickles, &c. Wax, Sperm and Composition Candles.

He continued in the business until his death in 1892.

Liberal in politics, Robert Forster was elected councillor for the North Ward in 1864 and re-elected in 1867. He was promoted to Alderman in 1869 and in November of that year was made Mayor of the Borough for the period 1869 to 1870. He was appointed a Justice of the Peace for the Borough in 1874 and in 1883 was elected to the North Riding County Council to represent Scarborough. He was again made Mayor of the Borough in 1884 for the period 1884 to 1885. During this mayoralty the Scarborough-Whitby Railway was opened in July 1885, a project with which Forster had been closely associated and in 1887 he became Chairman of the Board of Directors of the railway until his death in 1892. He was a Director and Trustee of Scarborough Savings Bank. He was a member of the Committee of the Cliff Bridge Company which managed Scarborough Spa and also a Scarborough Piers and Harbours Commissioner. He was elected a member of the Board of Guardians in 1882. He was also a Freemason.

Robert Forster never married but lived with his widowed sister Barbara Reid who came to Scarborough with him in 1846 and acted as his housekeeper. In 1891, ill-health forced him to resign his seat as Alderman after 25 years. He also resigned from the County Council and from the Board of Guardians. He became very ill in 1892, being attended regularly by Dr John Horne but died on 19 August 1892. After a service in All Saints' Church conducted by Rev. Frederick Holt, Robert Forster was buried in Scarborough Cemetery.

Further reading

Scarborough Gazette 25 August 1892 (Obituary)

Lidster, J. Robin, The Scarborough and Whitby Railway, Hendon Publishing, Lancs. 1977 (History of the railway)

FOWLER, Benjamin
1828 (Scarborough) - 1910 (Scarborough)

Mayor 1876-1877

Benjamin Fowler was born in Princess Street, Scarborough in 1828, the son of Henry Fowler JP, Collector of Her Majesty's Customs. Benjamin was educated at Scarborough Grammar School and went to sea in 1842 in the brig *Indus* commanded by his brother-in-law T. B. Walker, working mainly the Mediterranean trade. In 1851, Benjamin took command of the brig *Arnon* and began a series of voyages to Australia. It was in Tasmania, in 1852, that he married.

Fowler retired from the sea and settled back in Scarborough. He was first elected to the Town Council in November 1869 for South Ward and was re-elected in 1872, and 1875. He was made Mayor of the Borough for the period 1876 to 1877 and later elected Alderman. He finally retired from the Council in 1889. He held many public appointments including Chairman of the Board of Guardians (1884-1895), Trustee of the Municipal Charities, Trustee of Wilson's Mariners' Hospital and of the Old Savings Bank. He was a Commissioner of Income Tax, President of Scarborough Building Society, President of Scarborough Hospital and Dispensary, a member of the Committee of the Cliff Bridge Company which managed Scarborough Spa, Chairman of the Scarborough Gas Company and a Life Member of the Scarborough Harbour Commissioners. He was made a magistrate for the Borough in 1878 and for the North Riding in 1892. He was Chairman of the Licensing Justices until his death in 1910.

In 1852, Benjamin Fowler married Sarah, the eldest daughter of Captain William Neilly of Carrick Fergus, County Antrim, a veteran of the Peninsular and Waterloo Campaigns. Sarah was born in Tasmania where she and Benjamin were married. Their son, William Hastings Fowler (q.v.), was born in 1857 on the ship *The Henry Reed* while off the coast of Hastings when they were returning from Australia. William also became a Town Councillor and was made Mayor of the Borough in the presence of his father in November 1905.

Benjamin Fowler died at his home, *Weston House*, Westwood, Scarborough in July 1910, his wife having predeceased him. Benjamin was buried in Manor Road Cemetery after a funeral service at the Parish Church.

Further reading
Scarborough Mercury 15 July 1910 (Obituary)
Scarborough Pictorial 10 December 1913 (re his son W. H. Fowler)

FOWLER, Valentine
1849 (Filey) - 1918 (Scarborough)
Mayor 1894-1895 & 1907-1908

Valentine Fowler was born on 4 December 1849 in Filey, the son of Benjamin Fowler (q.v.), a Freeman of Scarborough who had moved there that year. Valentine was educated at a private school in Filey run by a Mr Clarkson. When he was 15, he was apprenticed to Benjamin Taylor, a chemist of Briggate, Leeds, where he worked as an assistant for two years. However, Valentine Fowler was struck down by typhoid and moved to Scarborough to convalesce. His uncle, also Valentine Fowler, was Secretary and Manager of the Scarborough Water Company and in 1869, the young Valentine joined the business. He worked there for ten years until it was taken over in 1880 by Scarborough Corporation. Valentine jun. then built up a flourishing business as an auctioneer and valuer in Scarborough.

At the age of 32, Valentine Fowler was elected to the Town Council as a Conservative for the South Ward in a by-election in 1881 and re-elected the following year. However, he was defeated three years later in the newly formed West Ward by the Liberal, William S. Rowntree, but was returned for the same Ward in November 1886. He was again defeated in the West Ward in 1889 but the following year was successful in the South Ward. Altogether he served on the Council for 32 years. He was made Borough Mayor for the period 1894 to 1895. One of the stranger functions he performed during his mayoralty was to approve four *Health Lectures to Women* to be given in February 1895 by Mrs Dr Longshore-Potts, over which the Mayoress presided. In 1896, he was appointed a Justice of the Peace for the Borough. He was re-elected a councillor in 1898 but defeated in 1901 after which he was made an Alderman and in 1907 he was again invited to be mayor. The major event of his second mayoralty was the opening of Marine Drive in August 1908 by HRH the Duke of Connaught, accompanied by the Duchess and the Princess Patricia.

Valentine Fowler was a Harbour Commissioner, Chairman of the Alexandra Hotel Company Ltd of Bridlington and held directorships of the Scarborough Daily Post, the Scarborough Tramways Company Ltd and the Savings Bank. He was also Secretary to the South Cliff Tramways Company Ltd.

Valentine Fowler was an active official of the Scarborough Conservative Association and for many years he was a director of the Constitutional (Conservative) Club. He was a churchwarden at All Saints' Church, Falsgrave and a Freemason, being a member of the Old Globe Lodge from 1873.

Valentine Fowler married Lizzie, daughter of Frederick Oates, of Farnham near Knaresborough in 1873. In 1917, their son, Major Valentine Fowler of the Yorkshire Regiment, was killed in action at Ypres, and was buried in Croisilles Cemetery in France.

Valentine Fowler died on 20 August 1918 at his home 13, Alma Square after a seizure. He was buried in Scarborough Cemetery on 23 August.

Further reading
Scarborough Pictorial 5 November 1913 (Biography)
Scarborough Mercury 23 August 1918 (Obituary)
Blakey, J.W. (ed.) Some Scarborough Faces, Past and Present, Scarborough Gazette Printing & Publishing Co. 1901 pgs 76 - 78 (Biography)
Scott, W. Herbert, ed. W. T. Pike, North and East Ridings of Yorkshire Contemporary Biographies at the Opening of XX Century, Brighton 1903 (Biography)
Who's Who – Yorkshire, 1912, Westminster Publishing Co. Ltd London.

FOWLER, William Hastings
1857 (at sea) - 1919 (Scarborough)

Mayor 1905-1906

William Hastings Fowler was born on 2
May 1857 on the vessel *The Henry Reed*
off Hastings when his parents, Benjamin
(q.v.) and Sarah Fowler, were returning
from Australia. His father, a Scarborough
ship owner, was in command of the
vessel, and made regular voyages between
England and Australia.

Before William H. Fowler was five years
old he had been around the world four
times. At the age of 17, in 1874, he was
articled to the Scarborough firm of
solicitors *Turnbull, Graham & Moody* and
qualified as a solicitor in 1879. He then
spent time in Chambers at Lincoln's Inn
with George Davidson, an eminent conveyance counsel. Fowler returned
to Scarborough in July 1880 and became a partner in the firm of *Messrs
Tate, Cook & Fowler* of Westborough which later became *Messrs Cook,
Fowler & Outhet* of York Place.

William Fowler was a member of Scarborough School Board from 1892 to
1895. He then decided to enter local politics standing unsuccessfully for
the Town Council in 1899 as a Conservative. However, in 1901 he was
elected for the South Ward and again in 1903. He was made an Alderman
in 1904 and made Mayor of the Borough for the period 1905 to 1906. As a
Town Councillor he was at various times Chairman of the Sanitary and
Lighting Committee, of the Parliamentary Bills Sub-Committee and of the
Marine Drive Sub-Committee (1902-1905). He was a life member Harbour
Commissioner, being chairman in 1913. Other public appointments
included being a director of the Scarborough Gas Company, a Trustee of
Wilson's Mariners' Asylum and a Trustee of the Municipal Charities.

In 1874, as he started his articles, Fowler had joined the local Rifle
Volunteers and had been promoted the next year to Sub-Lieutenant. After
30 years service, he retired in 1904 with the honorary rank of Lieutenant
Colonel. He was a warden of Christ Church, Scarborough, a trustee of the
York Diocesan Trust and a trustee of the Local Church Lands Trust.

William Hastings Fowler married Elizabeth Annie Candler, the daughter of Thomas Joseph Candler of the *Low Hall*, West Ayton, in July 1889. They had three children, two sons and a daughter. One son, Neilley Fowler, studied at Christ's College, Cambridge and was articled to his father's firm while the other, Kenneth Fowler, became an officer in the New Zealand Shipping Co. and was also an officer in the Royal Naval Reserve. Their daughter Katherine married Major Clive Taylor, the son of a local doctor, Dr Edward M. Taylor

William Hastings Fowler died of pneumonia on 4 June 1919 at his home, *Langford House,* Westwood, Scarborough.

Further reading
Scarborough Pictorial 10 December 1913 (Biography and portrait above)
Scarborough Mercury 6 June 1919 (Obituary)

GIBSON, Ambrose
1800 (Scarborough) - 1870 (Scarborough)
                                             Mayor 1864-1865 & 1865-1866

Ambrose Gibson was born in Scarborough in 1800 and became a plumber, glazier and gasfitter in the Town. By 1851, he employed one assistant and two apprentices. He appears to have continued the business at least until 1860 when his wife died. After this he retired and took an interest in municipal affairs.

Gibson became a member of the Board of Guardians and a trustee of the Municipal Charities. He was elected to the Town Council and in 1864 he was made Mayor of the Borough for the period 1864 to 1865 and re-elected for 1865 to 1866. During the first period of his mayoralty he authorised a grand civic procession across the newly opened Valley Bridge on 1 July 1865. In 1868, Gibson was appointed an Alderman.

Ambrose Gibson and his wife Eleanor had at least four children, three sons and a daughter. One son, William born c. 1828, became a chemist and druggist working in Bristol while another, Thomas Middleton, born 1831, became a master mariner. Their daughter, Sarah, born 1835, married Joseph Good of Hull in 1862. Ambrose's wife, Eleanor, died in 1860 after which he appears to have retired from business. Gibson was an influential member of the Wesleyan denomination and for a long period was a class-leader. From about 1866 to 1869 he held the office of Wesleyan Circuit-Steward.

Ambrose Gibson caught a chill at Scarborough Spa in September 1870 and died about four days later on 21 September at his home, 12, Alma Square. His medical attendants, Dr Richard Cross (q.v.) and Dr Richard Hutchinson, diagnosed *erysipelas of the mucous membrane of the left lung.*

Further reading
Scarborough Mercury 24 September 1870 (Obituary)

HAIGH, John
1802 (Halifax) - 1874 (Scarborough)

Mayor 1863-1864

John Haigh was born in Halifax in 1802 and became the head of a large manufacturing business in Huddersfield. He was Sub-Lieutenant of, and a magistrate for, the West Riding of Yorkshire. About 1858, he moved to Scarborough to live in the Crescent and was made a Justice of the Peace for both the Borough and for the North Riding.

John Haigh was elected to the Town Council as a Liberal member and, in 1863, was made Mayor of the Borough. He was later made an Alderman and retired from the Council about 1871. He was Chairman of the Cliff Bridge Company which managed Scarborough Spa and also President of Scarborough Cricket Club, of which he was a keen supporter. One of John Haigh's last acts was to sign Sir Harcourt Johnstone's (q.v.) nomination paper for the 1874 General Election as Scarborough's Liberal Parliamentary candidate.

John Haigh and his wife Mary (1810-1880) had at least six children including Fanny born 1829, John (1833-1868), Henry William (1834-1878) who became a doctor, Mary born 1844, Charles born 1846 and Walter.

John Haigh died at his home in the Crescent on 14 February 1874 having been in failing health for some time.

His widow, Mary, died January 1880 in London.

Further reading
Scarborough Mercury 14 February 1874 (Obituary)
Bayliss, A & P, The Medical Profession in Scarborough, 1700 to 1899, Scarborough 2005 (Son Dr Henry William Haigh)

HARLAND, William
1788 (Hartoft) - 1866 (Scarborough)
Mayor 1836-1837, 1842-1843 & 1848-1849

William Harland was born at Hartoft in the North Yorks Moors in 1788. He began his education at nearby Rosedale Abbey School and later in Scarborough, at John Hornsey's school in the Apple Market. He was apprenticed to a Scarborough chemist and druggist and by 1810 had his own business in Newborough.
William Harland then studied medicine and qualified from Edinburgh University in 1816 gaining his doctorate (MD) in 1820. He returned to Scarborough, setting up a medical practice in Newborough and establishing a suite of warm-water medicinal baths in Vernon Place. These became very popular and were extended in 1831.

HARLAND'S BATHS.

From an early age, Harland had exhibited a strong mechanical talent. As a boy he built a small limekiln to burn lime for his father's garden and he was a keen model maker. While a druggist's apprentice, he designed a machine to spread adhesive plasters and a device for making aerated waters. In 1827, he designed and patented a steam carriage to run on roads (Patent 1827 No. 5592). In collaboration with one of his sons, Edward James, he invented a tubular lifeboat.

In 1836, William Harland topped the poll in the South Ward in the first local elections held in Scarborough after municipal reform (see Introduction). He was elected Alderman for a period of six years and in November of that year he was made Scarborough's second Mayor. He remained a member of the Council and was re-elected Mayor for the period 1842 to 1843 and again for 1848 to 1849. St Mary's Parish Church had been restored from 1848 to 1850 and Dr Harland presented the glass for the east window of the newly restored church.

William Harland married Ann Peirson in June 1820 and they had several children. Their eldest son, William Aurelius, qualified in medicine from Edinburgh but, because he married a servant girl, had to leave England. He emigrated to Hong Kong where he became resident surgeon to the Victoria Seamen's Hospital but died there in 1858, aged 35. Another son, Edward

James became a shipbuilder in Belfast and founded the great *Harland & Wolff Company* while a third son, Albert Augustus, took Holy Orders.

Harland's wife Ann died in 1844. William Harland died in Scarborough on 6 April 1866, aged 79.

Further reading
Baker, Joseph Brogden, The History of Scarborough, London, 1882 pgs 447-448 (Biography)
Bayliss, A & P, The Medical Profession in Scarborough, 1700 to 1899, Scarborough 2005 (Biography)

HART, John
1822 (York) – 1897 (Scalby)

Mayor 1875-1876

John Hart was born in April 1822 in York, the fourth son of Thomas Hart, a mail guard. John was educated at the National School in York and then apprenticed to Mr Stansfield, a tailor in the City. Hart worked for a period in London and then in Darlington for two years before coming to Scarborough. Here he succeeded his brother, William Tasker Hart, *high class tailor* of 23, Newborough who had changed career to become an auctioneer and valuer. Their brother, James George Hart, was also an auctioneer in Scarborough.

In August 1870, John Hart was elected councillor for the North Ward, when Robert Forster (q.v.) was made an Alderman. When the Prince of Wales visited Scarborough in 1871, during the mayoralty of Dr Rooke (q.v.), the civic arrangements for the royal visit were delegated to Councillor Hart. John Hart was made Mayor of the Borough for the period 1875 to 1876. During his mayoralty, in 1876, there was a local petition to the Council to remove the Newborough Bar which was not, however, removed until much later. September 1876 was a memorable month in his mayoralty. Scarborough Spa was destroyed by fire, the Mayors of York, Liverpool, Stamford, Ripon and Richmond

made a formal visit to the Town as did the Duke of Cambridge, one of Queen Victoria's cousins. In 1884, the municipal wards of Scarborough had been re-arranged and Hart was defeated at the following election in 1886. He retired to Scalby, a village five miles North of Scarborough but carried on his business in the Town.

John Hart married Mary, the daughter of Captain Broches of Yarmouth. Their son James, born in 1847, became Rector of St Cuthbert's Church, Hawick while their daughter, Emily Jane (1858-1908) never married.

John Hart's wife, Mary, died suddenly on 7 December 1875, just after John had been made Mayor. He remarried, and with his new wife, Mary Ann, he had a daughter, Edith Mary, in 1881.

John Hart died in February 1897 and is buried in Scalby.

Further reading
Scarborough Gazette 18 February 1897 (Obituary)
Blakey, J.W. (ed.) Some Scarborough Faces, Past and Present, Scarborough Gazette Printing & Publishing Co. 1901 pgs 172-176 (Biography)

HEBDEN, Edward Hopper
1794 (Scarborough) - 1880 (Scarborough)

Mayor 1850-1851

Edward Hopper Hebden was born in Scarborough in 1794. In 1824, Hebden joined the *Old* Bank, Queen Street, Scarborough, which had been founded in 1788 as *Messrs Bell, Woodall & Co.* The partners were John Bell, John Woodall, James Tindall and Gowan Taylor, who had each subscribed £500 capital. By 1878, Edward Hebden had become the senior partner after the retirement of John Woodall (q.v.).

Edward Hopper Hebden was a member of the Old Scarborough Corporation being Senior Bailiff in 1826. In November of that year, Hebden laid the foundation stone for the Cliff Bridge. On its opening day it was reputed that he and John Woodall drove over it in a stage coach to assure residents of its stability. Hebden was the first chairman of the Cliff Bridge Company which owned not only the bridge but also Scarborough Spa. He was a director of the Company for almost 50 years, resigning after a major fire at the Spa in September 1876 because of a disagreement about what action should be taken over rebuilding.

Hebden was a Tory and was made a magistrate for the North Riding in 1833. When, in 1836, elections were first held for a reformed Scarborough Council (see Introduction) Hebden stood unsuccessfully for the North Ward, the liberal reformers taking 17 out of the 18 new seats. The only Tory elected was John Woodall (q.v.). Hebden was, however, elected to the Town Council in 1840. In 1850, he was made Mayor of the Borough for the period 1850 to 1851. At various times Hebden was a director of the Scarborough Public Market Company and was one of the first directors of the Scarborough Daily Post. At the time of his death, he was President of Scarborough Conservative Association.

In May 1818, Edward Hopper Hebden married Mary Tindall, sister of John Tindall one of the partners of the *Old Bank*. They had several children. One son, John, born 1823, qualified as a doctor and settled in Ripon after practising in Scarborough for a few years where he was surgeon to the Dispensary. Another son, Tindall Hebden married Jane Tindall, John Tindall's only daughter in 1858. A further son, William Hebden, born 1827, joined the bank in 1862 and later became its head. Their son, Edward, born 1829, was deaf and dumb. After the death of their parents, Edward was cared for in the family home by his unmarried sister Elizabeth, born 1826.

Hebden's wife Mary died in 1861 aged 68. Edward Hopper Hebden died on 3 November 1880, at his home, 6, Belvoir Terrace, Scarborough, aged 86. As the news of his death spread in the Town, the bells of Christ Church began to toll.

Further reading
Scarborough Mercury 6 November 1880 (Obituary)
Scarborough Pictorial 18 Feb 1914 (Biography)
Phillips, Maberly, History of Banks, Bankers and Banking, Northumberland, Durham & North Yorkshire, 1755-1894, London 1894 Pg 196 (History of the Bank)
Whittaker, Meredith, The Book of Scarborough Spaw, Barracuda Books Ltd, 1984 (History of Scarborough Spa)

HESP, John
1792 (Knapton) - 1860 (Scarborough)
Mayor 1837-1838, 1847-1848 & 1852-1853

John Hesp was born at Knapton, near Scarborough, in 1792. He became a solicitor and set up in practice in Tanner Street, now St Thomas Street, Scarborough. Later he went into partnership with John Uppleby and they were agents for the Yorkshire Insurance Company.

When, in November 1833, His Majesty's Commissioners visited to Town to assess whether Scarborough Corporation should be reformed (see Introduction), John Hesp was one of the three attorneys who challenged the Corporation's case to be left unchanged. The Commissioners found in favour of reform and John Hesp was elected under the Municipal Corporations Act to the first Town Council as a Liberal representative for the North Ward. He was made Mayor of the Borough for the period 1837 to 1838 and again for 1847-1848 and for 1852-1853. During this last mayoralty he officially opened Scarborough's new Market Hall.

John Hesp died on 28 September 1860, aged 69, at his house, 5, Westfield Terrace. His wife Rebecca died on 14 May 1864, aged 70. There is a marble memorial in St Mary's Church, Scarborough, to John and Rebecca Hesp.

Further reading
Binns, Jack, The History of Scarborough, North Yorkshire, Blackthorn Press, 2003 Chapter 12 (Reform of Scarborough Corporation)

HICK, Pantland
1833 (Scarborough) - 1900 (Scarborough)

Mayor 1883-1884

Pantland Hick was born in Scarborough in 1833, his father, also Pantland Hick, being a ship-owner. His mother, Mary, was the daughter of Burlinson Walker, another Scarborough ship-owner. Pantland Hick junior was educated at Scarborough Grammar School in King Street where the headmaster was Mr W. Merry. At the age of 14, Hick went to sea and later became master of several vessels working the Mediterranean, West Indian, Australian and East Indian trade. In 1863, Hick retired from the sea, returned to Scarborough and joined his father in the family shipping firm.

Pantland Hick was first elected to the Town Council in 1873 as a Liberal for the South Ward. He was re-elected in 1876, 1879 and 1882. In April 1882, it was reported that one of Hick's ships, the *Rochdale* was on fire in Sebastopol. In 1883, he was made Mayor for the period 1883 to 1884 and the following year was made an Alderman after the death of George Porrett (q.v.). Pantland Hick was re-elected to the Council in 1886 and 1892 finally retiring in 1898. As a councillor, Hick supported private enterprise against municipal expenditure. He therefore strongly opposed a proposal that the Council should erect a concert and recreation hall on the North Cliff. Hick was a Harbour Commissioner and Chairman of the Piers and Harbour Committee where his shipping knowledge was of great use. In 1886, he was appointed a Commissioner of the Peace for the Borough.

On 22 August 1863 in Liverpool, Pantland Hick married Ann, daughter of John Tindall, a ship-owner of *Knapton Lodge*, near Scarborough. They had no children.

Pantland Hick died at his home, 5, West Park Terrace, Falsgrave on 3 February 1900. He had been in failing health for three months and died of an attack of influenza. He was buried at Scarborough Cemetery after a funeral service at the Bar Congregational Church of which he had been a long time member. He was survived by Ann, his widow.

Further reading
Scarborough Mercury 9 February 1900 (Obituary)
Blakey, J.W. (ed.) Some Scarborough Faces, Past and Present, Scarborough Gazette Printing & Publishing Co. 1901 pgs 156-160 (Biography)

HOLDEN, William
1802 (Scarborough) - 1885 (York)

Mayor 1855-1856

William Holden was born in 1802, in Scarborough, where his father John ran a straw-hat manufacturing business in Newborough Street. For a period of time William took this over. However, by the mid 1840s, William

Holden was listed as running a free library from premises in Newborough and by 1851 Holden described himself as a *proprietor of houses.*

William Holden was elected a member of Scarborough Council in 1843 and retired in rotation in 1846 but he was not re-elected. However, in 1853 he was elected an Alderman and in 1855 he was made Mayor of the Borough for the period 1855 to 1856. In 1865, he was made a Justice of the Peace for Scarborough but he retired from all civic offices in 1871 because of failing health.

William Holden was married three times. His first wife Mary died in 1849, aged 47. His second wife, Hannah, died during his mayoralty in September 1856, aged 48. By his third wife, Mary, he had a daughter in 1861 who, in 1883, married F. W. Lowe, a Birmingham solicitor.

William Holden moved to York about 1877 where he died on 20 January 1885, aged 84. His body was brought back to Scarborough by train and he was buried in Dean Road Cemetery. The Mayor, Robert Forster (q.v.) and other civic dignitaries attended the funeral.

Further reading
Scarborough Gazette 29 January 1885 (Obituary)

HUTTON, James
1824 (Stanningly, Yorks) - 1893 (Scarborough)
Mayor 1888-1889 & 1889-1890

James Hutton was born in Stanningly, Leeds, in 1824 and, according to his obituary, was *of humble origin.* He came to Scarborough in the 1840s, where he set up as a grocer and corn dealer in St Thomas Street. He retired from business in the early 1870s and began to take an interest in public life.

> **J. HUTTON,**
> GROCER, TEA-DEALER, and Provision Merchant, No. 1, St. Thomas' Street, Scarbro'.
> *Families supplied with the best Cheshire and Derbyshire Cheese, Hams, Bacon, Lard, &c.—MALTON FLOUR.*

In 1872, Hutton stood for the North Ward but was defeated. However, he was successful the next year and he represented the Ward until the revision of wards in 1884. He was then returned for the newly created North-West Ward. In November 1888, he was made Mayor of the Borough for the period 1888 to 1889 at the end of which he became an Alderman. He was then made Mayor again for the following year, 1889 to 1890. During his mayoralty the Duke of Clarence, Queen Victoria's son, visited Scarborough to open the North Cliff improvements, there was a visit of the Channel Squadron to the bay and Lord Salisbury came to the Town to open the Constitutional (Conservative) Club. In 1889, Hutton was made a Borough Magistrate and in the same year he was elected a member of the Board of Guardians. He was also connected with the Charity Organisation Society, the Harbour Commissioners and the Savings Bank.

James Hutton married a Whitby lady, Hannah, in Christ Church, Scarborough on 12 June 1849, the Parish Church being closed at the time for restoration (1848-1850). They had five children who survived to adulthood. Their eldest son, Henry, born 1850, became a music teacher and organist at Albemarle Chapel. Their middle son, James Alfred, born 1866, qualified in medicine and practised in Scarborough until his death in 1930. Their youngest son, Thomas Fawcett, born 1867, studied at Scarborough School of Art but died suddenly and unexpectedly of heart disease at the age of 19. Of their two daughters, Hannah, born 1860, married W. W. Hopper, a Scarborough law stationer, while the other, Elizabeth, born 1858, remained unmarried and acted as housekeeper to her brother Dr Hutton.

James Hutton was taken ill on 15 October 1893 with chest pains after leaving Queen Street Wesleyan Chapel, of which he was a long standing member and a class leader. He was treated by his doctor son, James, but the next day he worsened and died of an aneurysm. His funeral service was held at Queen Street Chapel and was conducted by the Revs J. M. Wamsley, H. A. Scott & J. W. Simister. Alderman Hutton's family had asked that members of Scarborough Corporation should not attend the funeral in their civic capacity, but nonetheless many went in a personal capacity. Hutton's remains were buried in Scarborough Cemetery in the family vault.

Further reading
Scarborough Mercury 20 October 1893 (Obituary)

KNIGHT, Godfrey
1809 (Hesall) -1870 (Lockton)

Mayor 1861-1862 & 1862-1863

Godfrey Knight was born in Hesall in 1809. He came to Scarborough about 1844 and established himself as a successful brewer and maltster at

St Thomas's Brewery in North Street. In the mid-1860s, his son John joined him, the business becoming *G. Knight & Co.* However, in the late 1860s Godfrey Knight retired and George Lea joined the brewery which became *Knight and Lea.*

Knight's Brewery

Godfrey Knight entered local politics in 1852 when he was elected to the Town Council. In 1860, he was elected Alderman in succession to John Hesp (q.v.). Knight was made Mayor of the Borough for the period 1861 to 1862 and again for 1862 to 1863. Lord Londesborough (q.v. Denison) had married Lady Edith Somerset, the youngest daughter of the 7th Duke of Beaufort and when the couple first visited their house, *Londesborough Lodge,* in the Crescent, Godfrey Knight organised a public welcome in the form of a procession. There were fishermen and sailors carrying banners, local tenants of the Londesboroughs mounted on horseback, the band of the 6th North York Rifles, the Artillery Corps, the Rifle Corps and representatives of the Borough and of local Friendly Societies. Ten sailors on each side of the procession carried Union Jacks. Formal addresses were presented to and acknowledged by Lord Londesborough and the procession was said to have been the most extensive demonstration that had ever taken place in the Town. Knight's welcome for the couple was generously repaid by the Londesboroughs who became frequent visitors to Scarborough and supported many local activities.

Godfrey Knight and his wife, Mary, had three sons. The youngest son, also Godfrey, died at the age of seven in October 1858 and Mary Knight, died less than two months later, in December.

Godfrey Knight died suddenly and unexpectedly at Lockton near Pickering, on 12 August 1870. An inquest was held by the North Riding Coroner, John Ness, at the *Durham Ox* in Lockton. The medical evidence was that Knight had died of an apoplectic fit, the Coroner's verdict being *death by the visitation of God.* Knight's body was brought back to Scarborough by train and a large gathering attended the funeral including, the Mayor and Corporation. Shops along the route of the cortege were closed and Knight was interred in the family vault with the remains of his wife and youngest son following a service by Rev. Richard Blunt, Vicar of Scarborough. Godfrey Knight left two sons, one of whom was in America at the time of his father's death.

Further reading
Scarborough Mercury 16 August 1870 (Inquest)
Scarborough Mercury 20 August 1870 (Obituary)
Scarborough Mercury 20 April 1900 (Lord Londesborough's welcome procession)

LAND, William Charles
1828 (York) - 1908 (Scarborough)

Mayor 1878-1879

William Charles Land, born on 30 March 1828, was the third son of William, a York comb manufacturer and his wife Elizabeth. Young William was educated at Mr Crosby's school in York and in 1843, at age of 15, he was apprenticed to Thomas Cabry, engineer to North Eastern Railway Company. In 1852, Land took up a post with the South Eastern Railway Company in Ashford, Kent, but the next year the N.E.R. Company asked him to return to York to supervise a department in their engineering works. However, in 1854, Land visited Scarborough at a time when the Town was rapidly developing and decided that it offered him better opportunities. In 1855, he resigned his York railway post and set up as a grocer, spirits and wine merchant in South Street, South Cliff, Scarborough. His brother, John Birch Land, born in York in 1826, also moved to Scarborough where he set up as a builder and William invested significantly in his brother's housing development projects.

In 1874, on the advice of his GP, Dr William Taylor, W. C. Land semi-retired from his business but began to involve himself in public life in Scarborough. In November that year, Land was elected to the Town Council as a Conservative representative for the South Ward. In 1878, he was made Mayor of the Borough for the period 1878 to 1879 during which time he was Chairman of the Cliff Bridge Company. Land was a member of the Town Council for 21 years, 15 years as a councillor and six as an Alderman. In 1888, he was appointed a Magistrate for the Borough. He was a member of many different Council committees, over 40 in 1895. He

was Chairman of the Parks and Pleasure Grounds Committee from 1890 to 1895 at a time when the Council was beginning to beautify the Town. When the Council bought Scarborough Water Company, Land became a member of the Water Committee. He was also a Harbour Commissioner, a member of the Board of Guardians and a member of the School Board. He was a Director and Trustee of the Savings Bank, a Director of the South Cliff Tramway and of many other commercial bodies.

William Land was involved with St Martin's-on-the-Hill Church from its erection in 1863 and, from 1878, he was a churchwarden. Land was also a freemason, being a member of the Old Globe Lodge. In October 1903, Land was made a Freeman of the Borough of Scarborough at the same time as Earl Feversham and Henry Darley (q.v.). As William Land's father was a Freeman of York, William was also a Freeman of that City, by right of birth.

In 1851, William C. Land married Mary Winteringham, daughter of Robert Winteringham of Boroughbridge. They had one son William H. Land, born in Scarborough in 1859, who became a solicitor.

William Charles Land died in July 1908 at his home, *Waldeck House*, Grosvenor Crescent. He had been in failing health for some time and had just returned from visiting his son in Nuneaton. W. C. Land was buried in Scarborough Cemetery after a funeral service at St Martin's.

Further reading
Scarborough Mercury 31 July 1908 (Obituary)
Scarborough Pictorial 14 March 1914 (Biography)
Blakey, J.W. (ed.) Some Scarborough Faces, Past and Present, Scarborough Gazette Printing & Publishing Co. 1901 pgs 162-166 (Biography)

MARILLIER, Robert Aspland
1826 (Harrow) - 1903 (Torquay)

Mayor 1896-1897

Robert Aspland Marillier was born in Harrow in 1825 and received his initial education there. He was then articled to Thomas Wicksteed, a respected water engineer of London. Marillier had hardly completed his apprenticeship when he had an offer from Hull to take charge of the waterworks there. He took up the post in 1845 and stayed for the next 16 years. He then worked as engineer to the Hull Local Board of Health for four years before taking up the post of Engineer to the Hull Docks Company, which he held until 1893, when it was taken over by North Eastern Railway Company. While working for the Docks Company Marillier personally superintended the construction of Sir William Wright's Dock, St Andrew's (fish) Dock and two large graving docks. In 1884, he came to live in Scarborough and for the next nine years commuted to work in Hull. In 1890, he had a house built, *Holbeck Hurst*, Esplanade, designed by the Scarborough architects' firm, *Hall & Tugwell*. This was later bought and demolished by Alfred Shuttleworth to improve the southerly view from Shuttleworth's house, *Red Court*, so creating the Shuttleworth Gardens.

Robert Marillier became active in the Liberal Party in Scarborough as soon as he came to the Town. In a by-election in November 1895, he was elected Liberal councillor for the West Ward together with the other Liberal candidate, Meredith T. Whittaker. After only twelve months as a councillor, Marillier was made Mayor for the period 1896 to 1897. The year 1897 was Queen Victoria's Diamond Jubilee Year and Marillier was closely involved with celebrations in the Town. Together with other provincial mayors he was presented to the Queen on 23 June. The year was also marked by the presentation by Councillor Henry Darley (q.v.) of a chain of office to the Mayoress, Mrs Emma Marillier, and this has since been worn by her successors. During his mayoralty, Robert Marillier also laid the foundation stone of Marine Drive with great ceremony.

Although Robert Marillier lost his seat on Scarborough Town Council in 1898, in that year he succeeded John W. Woodall (q.v.) as Liberal representative of Scarborough's Central Ward on the North Riding County Council. From 1896 to his death in 1903 Robert Marillier was President of Scarborough Liberal Association.

In his retirement Robert Marillier spent the winter months in the South of England and the summer in Scarborough. For a period of time he owned a house in Hampstead but later moved to the Wellswood Hall Estate in Torquay. It was here in January 1903 that he developed a severe attack of influenza and pneumonia and died early in February leaving a widow, Emma, and a step-daughter.

Further reading
Scarborough Mercury 13 February 1903 (Obituary)
Blakey, J.W. (ed.) Some Scarborough Faces, Past and Present, Scarborough Gazette Printing & Publishing Co. 1901 pgs 184-188 (Biography)

MORGAN, William
1829 (Alrewas, Staffs) - 1907 (Scarborough)
Mayor 1902-1903, 1903-1904 & 1904-1905

William Morgan was born on 5 November 1829, in Alrewas, near Lichfield, Staffs. At an early age the family moved to Bradford where his father, John Morgan, was employed as a wool-comber. After leaving school, William Morgan had a series of jobs in Bradford, Lichfield and London where, at the age of 19, he took charge of a post-office receiving house in Fenchurch Street. He returned to Bradford where he bought a news stall on the railway station which later he sold to *Messrs W. H. Smith*. With the proceeds he opened a wholesale newsagent's business. This became a success, permitting him to  speculate in the theatrical and musical world and he went on to gain a wide reputation as theatre entrepreneur. In 1857, he brought to Bradford a performance of *Still Waters Run Deep* which had had a successful run in London. He was the first man to introduce Saturday Night Concerts into the provinces and this idea was soon copied in many other towns. He engaged many famous artists but offered prices to suit the pockets of the various classes who wanted to attend his productions - from three pence to one shilling and sixpence. One of his visiting artistes was Madame Adelina Patti (1843-1919) who was the most celebrated soprano of the time and was known as the *World's Queen of Song*. She refused to sing for the second night when she discovered that people in the gallery had only paid 3 pence. The resulting court case gave Morgan and his productions much useful publicity. In 1875, with some friends, he built the Princess's Theatre in Bradford which was unfortunately destroyed by fire three years later, Morgan loosing all his savings. Undaunted, he leased St George's Hall and the Mechanics' Hall for future concerts. A little later he was appointed manager of the Winter Gardens at Morecambe and a year later manager at the Winter Gardens at Blackpool, although he continued making all arrangements at Morecambe. Morgan instituted a ten-hour non-stop programme of entertainment at Morecambe and shares in the company rose from 10/- to £3-15/- each. He remained at Blackpool for seven years and then moved to Scarborough while still keeping his Blackpool interests.

In May 1886, Morgan and two associates bought the Aquarium at Scarborough for £5,150 including property and fixtures. The Aquarium had been built at a cost of £120,000 and had proved a white elephant. Morgan bought up shares in the company until he owned two thirds of the business. Five years later the Aquarium was floated as a limited liability company with a capital of £30,000 and until 1900 never paid less than a 10% dividend. Morgan was also Managing Director of Bridlington's People's Palace. In autumn 1904, he purchased Scarborough's North Promenade Pier at a public auction but it was washed away by a storm the following January. However, he rebuilt the entrance portion bordering on Clarence Drive as a seasonal place of entertainment. He also produced shows in the Exhibition Hall on Foreshore where the great height of the building was ideal for aerial performers on the flying trapeze.

When he settled in Scarborough, William Morgan had taken an interest in municipal affairs. In 1894, he unsuccessfully contested the Central Ward as a Conservative and was again unsuccessful the next year in East Ward. However, in 1902, the Town Council went outside its own body and invited William Morgan to be Mayor for the period 1902 to 1903, which he accepted. Morgan stood again as for the East Ward in November 1903 and this time he was successful. Now a Town Councillor, Morgan was again made Mayor for the period 1903 to 1904 and again for 1904 to 1905.

During his three periods as mayor there were a series of important events in Scarborough. In 1903, Princess Henry of Battenberg unveiled Queen Victoria's Statue and in the same year the Channel Fleet visited the Town and Morgan dispensed hospitality on a lavish scale. As Mayoress, Mrs

Morgan took a prominent role alongside her husband. In 1904, she formally opened the newly built Borough Sanatorium (today Cross Lane Hospital) and when, in the same year, the Electric Tramway was opened she drove the first tramcar. Also in 1904, Mrs Morgan laid the last stone of Marine Drive. She was a member of the Board of Guardians, a member of the Education Committee and she organised many charitable events in the Town. One popular event was tea and a concert for 400 fisher folk in the Old Town Hall at which each man received an ounce of tobacco from the Mayor.

William Morgan was married twice. His first wife, Eliza, died in the early 1880s. In September 1885, he married Octavia Flora, daughter of James Firth of Heckmondwike. Although they had no children, when William and Octavia moved to Scarborough they commissioned a local architect, Charles Edeson, to design a large villa as their family home - *Fairholme*, 9, Valley Road. Morgan also commissioned Edeson to design various developments at the Aquarium which included swimming baths in 1892 and a new theatre in 1895.

William Morgan died on 22 April 1907, at *Fairholme* and following a service at the Unitarian Church conducted by Rev. Otwell Binns he was buried in Scarborough Cemetery. The funeral was attended by a large number of people including most of the Corporation.

Further reading
Scarborough Mercury 26 April 1907 (Obituary)
Scarborough Pictorial 25 February 1914 (Biography)
Blakey, J.W. (ed.) Some Scarborough Faces, Past and Present, Scarborough Gazette Printing & Publishing Co. 1901 pgs 114-117 (Biography)
Scott, W. Herbert, ed. W. T. Pike, North and East Ridings of Yorkshire Contemporary Biographies at the Opening of XX Century, Brighton 1903 (Brief biography)

PIRIE, James
1838 (Scotland) - 1921 (Scarborough)

Mayor 1897-1998

James Pirie was born in 1838 in Keithall, Aberdeenshire. At the age of 19,

 he moved to Driffield, Yorkshire, to work for a drapery business. He later worked in the same trade in Hull for Robert Richie, as a travelling salesman between Driffield and Whitby. After three years, in 1860, he settled in Scarborough and set up his own travelling draper's business, first from Atlas Place and then from Castle Road. However, he later sold his business to James Brown. Pirie then held a series of jobs; he was a house agent, a district rate collector for the North Ward and later an auctioneer and commission agent. In 1883, he had a serious breakdown of health and sold this business to Andrew Orr. After recovering his health, he invested in a wide range of local companies of which he became a director. These included the Cliff Bridge Company, Scarborough Gas Company, Scarborough Public Market Company, the Central Tramway Company, Filey Water and Gas Company, Scarborough Laundry Company, Scarborough Building Society, the Public Baths Company and Scarborough Coffee House Company. He was secretary, and when it was wound up, liquidator of the Crown Hotel Company.

James Pirie was a Baptist and joined the Scarborough Ebenezer Church on his arrival in the Town. He became the Sunday School Superintendent. He was a keen missionary for the Baptists visiting many local villages and with John Waterworth he started a Sunday school at Burniston. Pirie was also a musician and was, with Dr John Naylor, a founder member of the Scarborough Choral Union.

James Pirie first stood as a Liberal candidate for the North Ward in 1886 but was defeated. However, he stood again in 1894 and was returned for North West Ward, a seat which he retained until 1906, in which year he was made an Alderman. He was made Mayor of the Borough for the period 1897 to 1898 and in the subsequent three years he was deputy mayor to Henry Darley (q.v.). In 1899, Pirie was made a Justice of the Peace for the Borough. Much of Pirie's work was done as Chairman of three important Council sub-committees, one for the Valley Bridge, one for the building of the Wykeham Street Bridge over the Scarborough and Whitby railway line and one for the building of new public (paying) urinals in the Town. James Pirie was a Harbour Commissioner, a member of the Board of Guardians for 17 years and he also held several offices in the Mechanics' Institute.

In July 1862, James Pirie married Hannah Collingwood Smailes, the daughter John Smailes, a Scarborough cabinet maker, at the Town's Baptist Chapel. They had no children. James Pirie died on 22 December 1921, aged 83, having been ill for most of that year and had resigned as an Alderman in November. His wife Hannah, also a life-long Baptist, died on 25 June 1922, aged 80. Mrs Pirie bequeathed their family house, 105, Castle Road, to the Baptist chapel to be its first manse with a legacy for its maintenance and also a further legacy to pay the salary of a Deaconess to work at the Ebenezer Church. There is a memorial window commemorating her generosity in the present-day Baptist Church in Columbus Ravine.

Further reading
Scarborough Pictorial 17 September 1913 (Biography)
Scarborough Mercury 23 December 1921 (Obituary)
Blakey, J.W. (ed.) Some Scarborough Faces, Past and Present, Scarborough Gazette Printing & Publishing Co. 1901 pgs 258-162 (Biography)

PORRETT, George
1818 (Scarborough) - 1884 (Scarborough)

Mayor 1874-1875

George Porrett was born in Scarborough in 1818. He was apprenticed to Samuel Turner, a local chemist and druggist and Porrett succeeded Turner in the shop at 64, Newborough.
Porrett added to the business an
agency for the County Fire
Insurance Company and an

> GEORGE PORRETT,
> CHEMIST AND DRUGGIST,
> 64, NEWBRO' STREET, SCARBOROUGH.

agency for the Chinese Tea Company. In the mid-1850s, he further diversified by entering into partnership with the ship-owner George Fenwick Brown. Their timber and raff merchants' business had sawmills initially at Bland's Cliff and later in Brook Street. George Porrett also became a ship-owner and engaged in the coal trade.

George Porrett, whose father had been a member of the old pre-1836 Corporation, was first elected to the Council in November 1859 for the

North Ward. In November 1868, he was elected Alderman in the place of George Willis (q.v.). Porrett was made Mayor of the Borough in November 1874 for the period 1874 to 1875. He was a member of the first School Board in 1871 and for many years was its Vice-Chairman. He was a Harbour Commissioner, Chairman of North Cliff Tramway Company, Manager and Secretary of the Public Swimming Baths, a Director of the Promenade Pier Company and a Borough Magistrate. A lifetime Wesleyan Methodist, Porrett held many offices in the church in Scarborough.

George Porrett and his wife Ann had several children. In 1875, during his mayoral year, their youngest daughter, Eliza, married Rev. W. H. Booth of London at Westborough Methodist Chapel. Their daughter, Annie Coulson, married James, the third son of Pantland Hick (q.v.) in 1869 and their daughter, Elizabeth Mary, married John Longbotham of Middleham in 1872. Their son, David, qualified as a solicitor and in 1880 married Emily, the daughter of Alderman Joshua Mountain of Sheffield. Their son, Thomas, worked in the timber trade.

George Porrett died suddenly and unexpectedly at his home in Belgrave Crescent, on Sunday 14 December 1884. He had earlier attended Westborough Methodist Chapel and also a Temperance Mission at the Old Town Hall. An inquest was held at Porrett's house by the Borough Coroner, Robert Collinson, and, based on Dr John Horne's medical testimony, a verdict of death by apoplexy was given. He was survived by his widow, Ann Herbert Porrett.

Further reading
Scarborough Mercury 19 December 1884 (Obituary)

PURNELL, Thomas
1799 (Scarborough) - 1856 (Scarborough)
Mayor 1839-1840 & 1845-1846

Thomas Purnell was born on 29 December 1799. By 1822 he had set up as a grocer and tea dealer in Newborough Street, Scarborough where he also had a stamp office.

Purnell was elected for the North Ward in the newly reformed Town Council at the first elections in 1836, representing the Liberal interest. In 1839, he was made Mayor of the Borough for the period 1839 to 1840, being the fifth to hold this office. During his mayoralty he laid the first stone of the Odd Fellows' Hall on 4 February 1840, which later became

Scarborough's Mechanics' Institute and is today Vernon Road Library. He was again Mayor for the period 1845 to 1846. He was also one of the Borough Magistrates.

Thomas Purnell married Jane Marshall Coulson and they had at least three sons and three daughters. Their two youngest sons both went to New Zealand. Thomas Augustus died there, aged 26, in 1861 while Aurelius returned to London in 1865 to marry Mary Rycroft Turner. He took her back to New Zealand where she died a year later. Purnell's second daughter, Jane Kirk Purnell, married the Scottish scientist, Sir David Brewster (1781-1868), at the British Consulate in Nice in 1857. In the same year their youngest daughter, Elizabeth Marshall Purnell, married a Royal Navy Surgeon, William Christy.

Thomas Purnell's wife, Jane, died on 5 March 1843, aged 42. In October 1847, Purnell married Ann Thompson, the daughter of a York solicitor, in Scarborough Parish Church.

Thomas Purnell died, aged 57 on 5 July 1856, at his Scarborough home, *Paradise House* and was buried at St Mary's Parish Church on 11 July.

Paradise House later became the Graham Sea Training and Engineering School but today has been divided into flats.

ROOKE, William Foster
1834 (Durham) - 1887 (Borrowdale)

Mayor 1870-1871 & 1871-1872

William Foster Rooke was born in Durham in 1834 and sometime before 1841 moved to Scarborough with his widowed father Charles, a physician, chemist and druggist. William studied medicine at Edinburgh University and first qualified in 1855. During the Crimean War he worked as an Assistant Surgeon in the Anglo-Turkish Army and published his reminiscences as a *Chapter from the Life of a Young Physician or Glimpses of Turkey & the Crimea 1855-1856.* After the War, Rooke completed his medical education and by 1858 he had set up as a physician in Scarborough. In the late-1860s, he took over his father's patent medicine business in the Town, which had worldwide sales.

The Rooke Family Business

Dr Rooke first became a member of the Town Council when he was elected for the North Ward in 1861. He was re-elected in 1864, 1867 and 1870. He was made Mayor of Scarborough for the period 1870 to 1871 and during his first week in office HRH the Prince of Wales visited the Town. Rooke was re-elected Mayor again for 1871-1872 and in November 1871 the Prince again visited, this time with the Princess of Wales. Rooke had delegated the arrangements for the Civic Reception to Councillor John Hart (q.v.). After this visit, the Prince developed typhoid fever caught, or so it was claimed, at Lord Londesborough's house in Scarborough.

There were several notable events during Rooke's mayoralty. Scarborough's first School Board was formed in February 1871, the first proposal to build Foreshore Road was put forward, the first telegraph message from Scarborough Post Office was sent on 19 August 1871, the first appointment of a Medical Officer for the Borough (Dr J. W. Taylor) was made on 25 March 1872, the Seamer Lane Gasworks were begun in May 1872, the building of the Scarborough-Whitby Railway started in July 1872 and in the same month the western portion of Scarborough Cemetery was opened. In September 1872, the Freemasons of Warwickshire presented the lifeboat the *Lady Leigh* to Scarborough. Rooke was Chairman of the Committee for the Relief of Distress in France during the Franco-Prussian War (1870-1871).

In his role as a local politician Dr Rooke was actively involved with many committees and he wrote several articles in the Scarborough Express on *National Emigration, National Education* and many others on social and political economy. He was also a prominent Mason and was installed as first master of Scarborough's *Star in the East Lodge no. 95* in November 1866.

In 1859, William Rooke married Jessie, the daughter of Alderman Bean of Scarborough. Rooke bought a considerable acreage of land, both in Yorkshire and in Cumbria. From 1877 onwards, he spent increasing time at his estate of *Manor House Grange* in Borrowdale, Cumberland. His wife Jessie died in January 1887 and William died on 8 November in the same year at *Manor House Grange* and was buried in Stornethwaite, Cumberland. Dr Rooke was survived by four daughters Lucy, born 1861, Emily, born 1862, Bertha, born 1869 and Sallah, born 1870.

Further reading
Scarborough Gazette 10 November 1887 (Obituary)
Bayliss, A & P, The Medical Profession in Scarborough, 1700 to 1899, Scarborough 2005

ROWNTREE, John Watson
1854 (Scarborough) - 1935 (Scarborough)

Mayor 1906-1907

John Watson Rowntree was born on 3 April 1854 in Scarborough where his father, John Rowntree, had a grocery business. J. W. Rowntree was one of the first pupils of Thomas Walton's School opened at 1, Belgrave Crescent, Scarborough in 1865 and he was still a pupil when the school transferred to Oliver's Mount. Rowntree continued his education at Bootham School, a Quaker institution in York. His brother Arthur, who edited a History of Scarborough in 1931, later became headmaster. On leaving school, John Watson Rowntree returned to Scarborough and was apprenticed to his father as a grocer and was later made a partner, becoming the senior partner, with his brother George, on death of their father. The Rowntrees added a café to their business which became an important feature of Scarborough life.

Rowntrees' Café

John Watson Rowntree was first elected to the Town Council in November 1889 as a Liberal for the East Ward. He was defeated in the elections of 1892 but successful one year later in the North West Ward. In November 1906, Rowntree was made Mayor of the Borough for the period 1906 to 1907 after which he was made an Alderman. He was Chairman of several Council Committees including the Watch Committee and the Streets and Buildings Committee. In the latter capacity he successfully sought a loan of £70,000 for the building of Marine Drive, a highly controversial project at time. He was present both at the laying of the foundation stone in 1897 and when the last stone was laid in 1904 by William Morgan's (q.v.) wife. He was also Chairman of the Finance Committee and for many years he was a member of the Harbour Commission of which he was elected a life member.

Rowntree was a life long supporter of the Adult School Movement and for many years held classes at the St Sepulchre Street Adult School. Supported also by his cousin, Joshua Rowntree (q.v.), the movement grew in Scarborough culminating with the building of the Roscoe Rooms in 1903 to accommodate increasing numbers. For many years John W. Rowntree was treasurer of the British and Foreign Bible Society, a supporter and past

87

president of the District Nursing Association and a strong supporter of the Temperance Movement.

Rowntree was a Quaker and a pacifist. In March 1900, during the Boer War, Joshua Rowntree organised a meeting of the local Peace Society to be addressed by J. Cronwright Schreiner (1863-1936), a British subject from South Africa who was on a lecture tour in England. The meeting was held in John Rowntree and Sons' Westborough Café. Incensed by this, a mob broke up the gathering causing great damage to the shop and went on to attack other Rowntree businesses and their private houses. At the time General Booth of the Salvation Army was a visitor at J. W. Rowntree's house.

After the First World War, John W. Rowntree joined the Labour Party, believing that it better reflected his views than the Liberal Party. He contested the General Election of 1918 as the first ever Labour candidate for the newly formed constituency of Scarborough and Whitby. He was unsuccessful and thereafter withdrew from local politics. In fact, the first successful Labour candidate for Scarborough was Lawrie Quinn elected in 1997.

John W. Rowntree died on Saturday night, 20 April 1935, at his home, *The Rowans*, Westover Road, Scarborough. He was 81 years old and had continued working in the family business up to a week before his death when he had a seizure. He was cremated at Hull Crematorium and his ashes were interred in the family grave in Scarborough Cemetery. There were two memorial services for him in Scarborough, one conducted by Mr Arnold Rowntree of York at the Friends' Meeting House and the other at the Bar Congregational Church.

In 1855, John Watson Rowntree had married Eliza Gravely, the daughter of Frederick Gravely of Wellingborough. Eliza survived John as did their son, Harold Rowntree, and their daughter Kathleen, Mrs Burleigh Fincken.

Further reading
Scarborough Pictorial 17 December 1914 (Biography)
Scarborough Evening News 22 Apr 1935 (Obituary)

ROWNTREE, Joshua
1844 (Scarborough) - 1915 (Scalby)

Mayor 1885-1886
Scarborough MP (Liberal) 1886-1892
(This entry is repeated in the section on MPs)

Joshua Rowntree, born on 6 April 1844, was the son of John and Jane Rowntree, Quaker grocers of Scarborough. In his early years, Joshua, together with his sisters, was educated at home by a governess. He then went to Bootham School, a Quaker institution in York and later was articled to a solicitor in that City. After this he gained legal experience in London in the chambers of Sir E. Fry. In 1866, Rowntree returned to Scarborough to join the local solicitor, William Drawbridge, initially as a junior partner.

While in London, Joshua Rowntree had heard a speech by Earl Derby in the House of Lords. Derby had claimed that the declaration made by non-Anglican town councillors, that they would not injure the Establishment, was not worth the paper it was written on. Incensed by this, Rowntree joined the Liberation Society and thus began a life in Liberal politics. On his return to Scarborough, Rowntree was instrumental in the beginnings of adult education in the Town, a movement with which he was associated for the rest of his life. Scarborough's first Adult School was held in an old sail loft in Courtin Steps, Eastborough but grew rapidly and moved to larger premises in Spring Gardens in 1871 and then to new premises in St Sepulchre Street in 1894. The movement continued to grow and in 1903 Joshua Rowntree laid the foundation stone for the new Adult School in Roscoe Street. The movement included a rowing club which became Scarborough Rowing Club, a sick club and a Coffee Cart Company which became the Scarborough Coffee House Company (a temperance movement).

In 1868, Scarborough Council resolved to sell off the Old Town Hall in St Nicholas Street to a bank, a move resisted by many townsfolk. A committee was set up to oppose the sale and Joshua Rowntree was appointed secretary. The Local Government Board refused to approve the sale until after the November local elections of that year. The proposal was defeated when opponents were returned for the South and North Wards,

89

and the building was converted into a public meeting room with shops below.

In 1878, Joshua Rowntree agreed to stand as a Liberal candidate for Scarborough Council, although he refused to canvass. He and William Barry (q.v.) were elected by a large majority to represent the South Ward. When Scarborough's two wards were divided into six, Rowntree stood as candidate for the East Ward but lost by just one vote. However, two months later a vacancy occurred in the same Ward and he was returned with a majority of 86. This was his last municipal contest. He was made Mayor of the Borough for the period 1885 to 1886, having first explained that he would not attend church in state or give the usual grand municipal banquet. Instead, he entertained members of the Council to dinner, without wine, and a larger number of guests at two soirées at the Grand Hotel. In Scarborough, Rowntree was a Borough magistrate, a Harbour Commissioner and sat on the School Board.

In 1886, during Rowntree's mayoralty, Gladstone was defeated over home-rule for Ireland which precipitated a general election. In order to stand as Scarborough's Liberal home-rule candidate for Parliament, Joshua Rowntree resigned as Mayor, incurring a £50 penalty. He was successful in the general election of 3 July 1886, getting 2,122 votes ousting Sir George Sitwell (q.v.), the sitting member, who got 2,020. In fact, Scarborough was one of only two Liberal gains in that election. The Conservatives formed a coalition with the Unionist Liberals forming an anti-home-rule administration. Rowntree remained member for Scarborough until 1892 when Sitwell re-took the seat. Rowntree was a staunch promoter of women's rights, amongst other things helping Florence Balgarnie, daughter of the local Congregational minister, to get elected to the first School Board in 1870 and another lady to be elected to the Board of Guardians in 1872.

Joshua Rowntree married Isabella Tindall, the eldest daughter of Robert Tindall (q.v.) in September 1880, away from Scarborough at the Friends' Meeting House in Ilkley. The Tindalls were Quaker ship owners who had been disowned by the Friends when, on the demand of their crews, they had armed their vessels against pirates. They were also Tories and the marriage away from Scarborough was said to save any embarrassment. Nonetheless, Joshua and Isabella returned to the Town to live in *Rawdon Villas*. Their only son Maurice was born in 1882. After being unsuccessful in the general election of 1892 Rowntree spent time travelling, visiting, amongst other places, Palestine in 1898, and Australia, New Zealand, and the United States in 1902-1903.

During the Boer War, Joshua Rowntree looked for ways to promote conciliation and peace. He organised a pro-peace meeting in Scarborough in March 1900 to be addressed by S. Cronwright Schreiner (1863-1936) a British subject from South Africa who was on a lecture tour in England. This resulted in mob violence against the Rowntree families and their properties, needing the local militia to disperse the rioters.

Damage to Rowntrees' Grocers

Between December 1900 and April 1901, Joshua Rowntree, his wife and nephew Harold T. Ellis (1875-1930), visited South Africa to investigate possible Quaker relief work, particularly in the concentration camps. Amongst the contacts they made there was a young Indian barrister, Mr Gandhi, who told them of the demoralising conditions to which all Asian people were subjected.

In 1912, Joshua Rowntree and his son rented *Worfolk*, a cottage near Staintondale owned by the Quakers. Joshua spent more and more time there until 1914, when, after a spell in a nursing home, he moved to *Wrea Head*, Scalby, where Maria Ellis, his widowed sister, lived. Joshua Rowntree died there in his sleep on 9 February 1915. He was survived by his widow and their only son Maurice Lotherington Rowntree.

Further reading
Scarborough Mercury 4 November 1892 (Address by Rowntree to Scarborough Women's Liberal Union)
Scarborough Pictorial 22 October 1913 (Biography)
Scarborough Mercury 12 February 1915 (Obituary)
Oxford Dictionary of National Biography
Binns, Jack, Heroes, Rogues and Eccentrics, A Biographical Journey Through Scarborough's Past, Blackthorn Press, 2002 pgs 200-208 (biography)
Binns, Jack, The History of Scarborough, North Yorkshire, Blackthorn Press, 2003 pgs 225-226 (Schreiner riots)
Robson S.E. Joshua Rowntree, George Allen & Unwin, London 1916 (Biography)
Rowntree, Arthur (ed.), The History of Scarborough, J. M. Dent, London 1931 pgs 307-398 (Schreiner riots)
Who's Who – Yorkshire, 1912, Westminster Publishing Co. Ltd London

SHARPIN, John Fairgray
1821 (Ripon) - 1895 (Scarborough)

Mayor 1853-1854

John Fairgray Sharpin was born in March 1821 in Ripon. His two grandfathers had both been mayors, his maternal grandfather, Alderman Fairgray in Ripon in 1806 and his paternal grandfather, William Sharpin, in Grantham in 1763. John Sharpin began school in Ripon but later was educated firstly by Rev. James Newsam, at Sharrow Parsonage and then by Rev. John Husband at Whixley Vicarage. He then worked for two years for an uncle who was a grocer and tea dealer.

In 1844, John Sharpin visited his brother, Hesseltine, who was living at that time in Scarborough (Mile End Place, Falsgrave) but later moved to run the Brunswick Hotel in Harrogate. The Crown Hotel in Scarborough had just being completed and in 1845, at the age of 24, J. F. Sharpin took a twelve year lease on the premises. He built up the business so that the Crown Hotel became one of the major attractions of the Town. In 1856, he bought two old houses in Huntriss Row and erected premises known as the Assembly Rooms. These were made available for functions such as auctions, concerts, exhibitions, lectures etc. and also incorporated a billiards hall and a photographic gallery. In 1857, his lease on the Crown Hotel ended and he sold all of the hotel contents, the sale taking 31 days. On leaving the hotel, Sharpin and his wife were presented with silver dishes by near neighbours and friends and Scarborough Corporation presented them with a magnificent silver vase made in the Town by *Bright & Son*. Sharpin then spent several years in London as a partner in a wine and spirits business. In the mid-1860s, he returned to Scarborough and opened a similar business in his

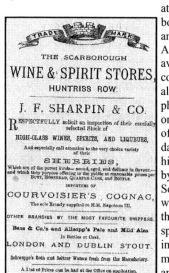

Assembly Rooms. One of his valuable customers was Edward, Prince of Wales and he was allowed to display the Prince's Coat of Arms. In 1879, John Fairgray Sharpin sold this business to Charles Laughton and moved to Ripon. However, by 1890, the Sharpin family had returned to Scarborough to live at 10, York Place.

In 1851, John F. Sharpin was elected to the Town Council and in November 1853, he was made Borough Mayor for the period 1853 to 1854. At the time he was said to be the youngest mayor in England at the age of 32. He is also reported to have given the first Civic Banquet *worthy of the name*. Sharpin was respected for having brought many wealthy visitors to Scarborough, thereby improving the Town's economy. In 1867, he was appointed a Borough Magistrate and was President of Scarborough Licensed Victuallers Association from its formation.

John Sharpin was married twice. His first wife, Jeanette, died aged 36, in 1861. Sharpin erected a memorial to her in Scarborough Cemetery. This comprised a fluted granite column bearing a bronze medallion image of his wife taken from a pen and ink sketch by the Swiss artist Francis Buchser. In 1866, John Sharpin married Mary Alice Atkinson at All Saints' Church in Islington. He had children by both wives.

John Fairgray Sharpin died very suddenly at his home, 10, York Place on 11 June 1895, although he had been in failing health for the previous three years. Death was reported to have been due to internal haemorrhage.

Further reading
Scarborough Mercury 14 June 1895 (Obituary)
Blakey, J.W. (ed.) Some Scarborough Faces, Past and Present, Scarborough Gazette Printing & Publishing Co. 1901 pgs 144-150 (Biography)
The Crown Hotel Scarborough, 150 Years of Hospitality, 1995 Scarborough Library ref no. 647.9442 (History of the Crown Hotel)

SINFIELD, Joseph
1842 (Scarborough) - 1919 (Scarborough)

Mayor 1901-1902

Joseph Sinfield was born in November 1842 in Scarborough. He was apprenticed to a hairdresser in the Town and when he had finished his articles he set up his own business at 77, Newborough in 1862. This he developed and diversified becoming a major wholesale and retail confectioner. At the height of his business his main premises were still in

Newborough, but he had a wholesale warehouse in St Thomas Street and branch stores in St Thomas Street, Victoria Road, Sandside, Westborough, Cliff Parade, Castle Road, Huntriss Row and at Scarborough Aquarium.

Joseph Sinfield was first returned to the Town Council as a Liberal for the Central Ward in 1893 when he defeated the Tory brewer, Herbert A. Hudson, the sitting member. He was again returned, unopposed, in 1896 and retained his seat in 1899 in a contested election, his opponent being William Hastings Fowler (q.v.). Sinfield was made Mayor of the Borough for the period 1901 to 1902. During his mayoralty there was the coronation of King Edward VII and also the close of the South African War. Sinfield was closely involved with municipal celebrations both for the Coronation and for the return of the local Volunteer Corps from the front. In 1902, he was appointed a Borough magistrate although he was defeated in the local elections of the same year. Sinfield did not stand again as a Councillor but he was Deputy Mayor to William Morgan (q.v.) during his mayoralty, 1904 to 1905.

Joseph Sinfield was associated with a number of local enterprises including the Cliff Boarding House Company, the Scarborough and District Bill Posting Company, the Plate Glass Insurance Company, Scarborough Liberal Club and Scarborough Hospital and Dispensary. He was also a Trustee of the Municipal Charities. Sinfield was a staunch Wesleyan Methodist and held every office available to a layman at Queen Street Methodist Chapel.

JOSEPH SINFIELD'S

WHOLESALE AND RETAIL

Tobacco and Confectionery Stores,

76, 77, & 78, NEWBOROUGH STREET,

BRANCH STORES:
57, ST. THOMAS STREET.
56, VICTORIA STREET,
DIRECTLY OPPOSITE THE SPA HOTEL,
24, SANDSIDE,
41 and 42, WESTBOROUGH,
10, CLIFF PARADE,
77, CASTLE ROAD,
And CENTRAL TRANSEPT AT THE
PEOPLES' PALACE AND AQUARIUM.
SCARBOROUGH.

SHOPS SUPPLIED AT LOWEST PRICES.

In April 1867, Joseph Sinfield married Mary Elliot Turton, daughter of Matthew Turton of Esplanade, Scarborough. They had six children, four sons, John, Joseph, Walter and Joshua and two daughters, Mary and Alice. By 1891 John was an assistant in his father's business while Joseph and Walter were apprentice tobacconists.

94

Joseph Sinfield died on 21 November 1919 and was buried in Scarborough Cemetery after a funeral service at Westborough Wesleyan Methodist Church.

Further reading
Scarborough Pictorial 3 June 1914 (Biography)
Scarborough Mercury 28 November 1919 (Obituary)
Blakey, J.W. (ed.) Some Scarborough Faces, Past and Present, Scarborough Gazette Printing & Publishing Co. 1901 pgs 196-200 (Biography)
Scott, W. Herbert, ed. W. T. Pike, North and East Ridings of Yorkshire Contemporary Biographies at the Opening of XX Century, Brighton 1903.

SMITH, Benjamin
1808 (Temple Newsam) - 1898 (Scarborough)

Mayor 1877-1878

Benjamin Smith was born on 5 November 1808 at Temple Newsam, near Leeds, *the offspring of poor parents*. At an early age he was apprenticed to a brick-maker and after completing his articles came to Scarborough in 1834, aged 26. He worked for the Scarborough brick manufacturer and builder John Barry (q.v.) and was appointed his foreman, a post he held for 15 years. In 1850, Smith set up on his own account when he purchased a brick yard on South Cliff and also began business as a building contractor. However, at this time he also ran a cod-liver oil manufacturing business. His building business grew and by 1861 he employed 50 men. Later, in the 1860s, his son Samuel North Smith (q.v.) became a partner, the firm becoming *Benjamin Smith & Son*, builders.

A Liberal, Benjamin Smith was first elected to the Town Council in November 1861 as a representative for the North Ward. He was defeated in 1864 but in 1865 was elected for the South Ward. In 1877, he was made Mayor of the Borough for the period 1877 to 1878 but immediately upset several people when, as a total abstainer, he refused to have any alcohol at his inauguration banquet. However, others congratulated him on having the courage of his convictions. During his mayoralty he conducted a poll as to whether the local authority should purchase the Water Works. Votes in favour were 1845 with 845 against and the purchase went ahead. Also during his time as Mayor, the Duke of Cambridge visited Scarborough. Smith was defeated in the 1881 local elections and, having given 19 years service to the Town, he retired from public life.

In 1832, Benjamin Smith married Elizabeth Coates and they had two children, a daughter Annie Elizabeth who married Benjamin Wood, a Bradford merchant and a son, Samuel North Smith (q.v.) who, like his father, became Mayor of Scarborough. Benjamin Smith's wife died in 1868, aged 68. Smith re-married but his second wife, Martha, predeceased him. Smith was an active Wesleyan Methodist throughout his life, being a lay preacher in Scarborough and the neighbouring villages for 62 years. When he was 88 years old he preached his 56th anniversary sermon at Flamborough.

Benjamin Smith died a widower on 17 October 1898, at his home, 4, Beulah Terrace, Scarborough, aged 89. He had been ill for two weeks having been suffering from Bright's disease. A funeral service was conducted at Westborough Methodist Chapel attended by members of the Corporation and many local Wesleyan preachers.

Further reading
Scarborough Mercury 21 October 1898 (Obituary)
Blakey, J.W. (ed.) Some Scarborough Faces, Past and Present, Scarborough Gazette Printing & Publishing Co. 1901 pgs 190-194 (Biography)

SMITH, Hodgson
1808 (Scarborough) - 1892 (Scarborough)

Mayor 1858-1859

Hodgson Smith was born on 15 July 1808 in Cooks Row, Scarborough. He did not meet his father until he was seven years old as the latter, a sailor, had been incarcerated by the French during the Napoleonic Wars. At the age of twelve, Hodgson Smith went to sea and became a master mariner before he reached the age of 21.

He retired from the sea about 1841 but did not return to Scarborough until 1850 when he described himself as a ship-owner and began to take interest in the affairs of the Town. In 1857, he was elected Conservative councillor for the South Ward and in November of the next year he was made Mayor of the Borough for the period 1858 to 1859. He retired from Scarborough Council in 1866 and in 1868 was made a Borough JP. He was a Harbour Commissioner, a member of the Burial Board from 1857, a Trustee of the Seamen's Hospital, a Vice President of the Yorkshire Penny Savings Bank and a member of the Committee of the Cliff Bridge Company which managed Scarborough Spa. Hodgson Smith lived in Falsgrave and was a Churchwarden of nearby All Saints' Church from its opening in 1868 until he retired from the post in April 1887.

In 1839, Hodgson Smith married a Scarborough lady, Jane Margaret Halliday and they had five children. The eldest, Samuel, born 1846, became a master mariner, but while he was captain of the barque *Annie* he sailed to Australia and died there in August 1871. Another son, Walter, born 1856, also became a master mariner while a third son, Alfred Hodgson, born 1849, became a fancy goods dealer in Harrogate. One daughter, Jane Helena, born 1851, married Robert Sutherland Walker in 1876 but was widowed soon after. The other daughter, Annie, born 1851, was unmarried and was living at home, together with her brother Walter, at the time their father's death.

Hodgson Smith died a widower on 28 October 1892, at the age of 84 at his home, *Ednell House*, Falsgrave. He had been suffering from pneumonia. A funeral service was conducted at All Saints' Church by Rev. Robert Brown-Borthwick, assisted by the Right Rev. the Bishop of Hull, Richard Blunt who had previously been Vicar of Scarborough. Hodgson Smith was buried in Scarborough Cemetery. The funeral was attended by the Mayor, Lieut. Col. Steble (q.v.), and members of the Corporation, however, as the funeral was held on a polling day some members were unable to attend.

Further reading
Scarborough Mercury 4 November 1892 (Obituary)

SMITH, Samuel N.
1840 (Scarborough) - 1924 (Scarborough)

Mayor 1879-1880

Samuel North Smith was born in Scarborough in 1840, the son of Benjamin Smith (q.v.), a local builder and brick and tile manufacturer. Samuel joined his father's business which by 1867 was known as *Benjamin Smith & Son*. By the beginning of the 1880s, Benjamin had retired and Samuel was now in charge of the business which employed 35 men and 15 boys. As a builder, he was involved with the development of the Seamer Road Estate,

Oak Road and the neighbouring area where he lived at *Burleigh House*, 1, Highfield. He also owned other house property in the area. However, by the 1890s he changed career and became an accountant and estate agent.

Samuel North Smith, a Liberal, was unsuccessful when he first stood for the Town Council in 1874 but was elected as a representative for the North Ward in November 1877. Thus, for the next four years he and his father were both town councillors. Samuel was re-elected in 1880, 1883 and again in 1886, the first election after the division of town into six wards, when he represented the new Central Ward. He was defeated in 1889 by William Tonks but was successful in a by-election in same ward the next year. In November 1879, he was made Mayor of the Borough for the period 1879 to 1880. During his mayoralty, the Lord Mayor of London paid a formal visit to Scarborough to re-open Scarborough Spa which had been destroyed by a fire in 1876. In October 1881, Smith was appointed a Borough Magistrate and in February 1911 he succeeded Benjamin Fowler (q.v.) as chairman of Licensing Justices. Smith had an interest in a number of local companies including being a director of the South Cliff Tramway Company and Secretary and Director of the Southland's Boarding House Company which had premises on West Street.

Samuel Smith was a Wesleyan Methodist and was long associated with the Falsgrave Wesleyan Chapel where he held various offices including being secretary and treasurer.

Samuel Smith married Elizabeth Jane, daughter of Richard Spink, a Scarborough butcher, in June 1862. They had three sons and two daughters. Their eldest son, Stanley North Smith, became a chartered accountant working in Scarborough for some years before moving to Bristol. He also had been in charge of a section of the local Volunteers. Another son, Dr William North Smith, became a doctor of medicine but predeceased his father. There was a third son, Norman North Smith and two daughters Annie and Caroline. Elizabeth, Samuel's wife, predeceased him and he re-married.

Samuel North Smith died on 1 February 1924 at the *Southlands Boarding House*, Scarborough. He had been in ill health for some time and had fallen in his bedroom some three weeks earlier suffering an injury to his foot. There were complications and it became necessary to operate. However, his condition became critical and he did not regain consciousness before he died. His funeral service was held at the Falsgrave Wesleyan Methodist Chapel.

Further reading
Scarborough Mercury 8 Feb 1924 (Obituary)

SPURR, Henry
1796 (Doncaster) - 1865 (Scarborough)

Mayor 1857-1858

Henry Spurr was born in Doncaster in 1796 and retired to Scarborough in the early-1850s. He described himself as a landowner. He was elected a Town councillor and in November 1857 he was made Mayor of the Borough for the period 1857 to 1858. An early duty was officiating at the Parliamentary by-election in December 1857 when John Dent Dent (q.v.) was elected MP in place of Earl Mulgrave (q.v.)

Henry Spurr married Louisa Amelia and they had at least two children who accompanied them to Scarborough, a daughter, Harriet, born in Gainsborough in 1829 and a son James Frederick, also born in Gainsborough 1822. James qualified as a solicitor and by 1855 had set up in practice in Scarborough. A year later, he married Laura Radley in London.

Henry Spurr died on 30 April 1865, at his Scarborough home, *Westfield House*, 4, Westfield Terrace, aged 69.

STEBLE, Richard Fell
1836 (Lancs.) - 1899 (Scarborough)

Mayor 1891-1892
Scarborough MP (Liberal) 1884-1885
(This entry is repeated in the section on MPs)

Richard Fell Steble was born on 15 September 1835, the son of Rev. J. H. Steble BA of Cambridge, formerly of Whicham, Cumberland. Richard was educated at Rossall College near Fleetwood. He qualified as a solicitor in 1858 and went into practice in Liverpool. In August 1859, he joined the First Lancashire Rifle Volunteers and moved through the ranks becoming Lieutenant Colonel in 1867, a position he held until 1876.

In 1867, Richard Steble was elected a Conservative councillor for North Toxteth, Liverpool and served on the City Council for 14 years. He was Mayor of Liverpool in 1874 and in 1875. During his mayoralty, the Lord Mayor of London visited the City with other mayors. Steble made a gift to

Liverpool of a large fountain which was centrally placed in Lime Street near St George's Hall, the Art Gallery and Museum. In recognition of this a street was named after him.

In 1881, Steble came to live in Scarborough and soon entered local public life. In 1884, the Right Hon. J. D. Dodson (q.v.), the MP for Scarborough, was elevated to the peerage. In spite of having been a Conservative councillor in Liverpool, Steble was invited to contest the seat for the Liberals in the by-election of November of that year. He was successful against the Tory candidate, Sir George Sitwell (q.v.). However, Steble did not seek re-election in 1885 because of indifferent health and Sitwell won the seat.

Although not a member of Scarborough Council, Richard Steble was invited to become Mayor of the Borough in 1887 but he declined because of a recent accident. However, when invited in 1891, he did accept. His mayoral year was one long round of hospitalities, rich and poor being feted. He and his wife entertained 700 aged poor at the Grand Hotel at Christmas and they held an *At Home* in the Hotel which was attended by 900 guests. The Stebles held a series of popular concerts in the circus in St Thomas Street and as many as 2,000 attended the last one after which they entertained all of the artistes. Scarborough's cabmen, railwaymen and bath-chair men, together with their wives and children, were all entertained by the Mayor and his wife. On arrival in Scarborough, Steble was a Justice of the Peace for Liverpool and he became a JP for Scarborough and also for the North Riding. He was one of founders of the Scalby and Newby Agricultural Society and was President in 1899.

Richard Fell Steble was twice married. In June 1864, he married Elizabeth, the second daughter of John Garratt of Holywath, Coniston. Elizabeth died in May 1880. Steble then married Lily, the widow of John Metcalf of Pirzett, near Kendall by whom he had one daughter. His stepdaughter, Miss Metcalf-Steble, married Lieutenant Stansfeld, the adjutant of the local volunteers.

Richard Fell Steble died on 8 October 1899 at his residence *Ramsdale Bank*, 5, Belmont Road, Scarborough. He had suffered with sciatica while spending the summer at his country residence *The Knoll*, Bowness-on-Windermere. At the end of September he had had an apoplectic seizure but with treatment by Scarborough doctors Everley Taylor and Godfrey, Steble made a recovery. However, he had a second seizure on Sunday 8 October which was immediately fatal.

Richard Fell Steble was buried in Scarborough cemetery after a funeral service in Christ Church which the Mayor, Henry Darley (q.v.) attended along with most of the Corporation. In 1901, Steble's widow presented a Röntgen (X) Ray Apparatus to Scarborough Hospital and Dispensary in her husband's memory. Steble had been President of the Hospital in 1888, seven years before the discovery of X-rays by Wilhelm Konrad von Röntgen.

Further reading
Scarborough Mercury 13 October 1899 (Obituary)
Bayliss A. & P. & Jackson A., Scarborough Hospital and Dispensary, The First Fifty Years 1852-1902, Scarborough 2006 (Steble's involvement with the hospital)

TINDALL, Robert
1790 (Scarborough) - 1871 (Scarborough)
Mayor 1840-1841, 1841-1842, 1843-1844, 1846-1847 & 1849-1850

Robert Tindall was born in Scarborough in 1790 into an influential Quaker ship-owning and ship-building family. The Tindalls had built ships in Scarborough from the days of Oliver Cromwell. From the mid-1700s to the mid-1800s it was estimated that they had built about 200 ships in their yards in Scarborough. These ranged from 200 to 1,000 tons, many being regarded as models of naval architecture of their time. Robert, together with other members of the Tindall family managed the Sandside business which, by 1851, was employing 44 men. Richard Tindall, a nephew of Robert, later became the head of the firm. However, when Richard died, aged 37, in 1861, Robert, now aged 72, felt he was too old to take over the business which was closed soon after.

Tindall's Yard c. 1863

For many years before the Municipal Corporation Reform Act of 1836 (see Introduction), the Tindall family had been well represented on the Old Scarborough Corporation. However, in spite of his family involvement with the Old Corporation, Robert Tindall was elected to the newly reformed Town Council in 1836 as a Liberal representative for the South Ward. Robert was already involved in Scarborough affairs. In 1828, he was chairman of the building committee for the Rotunda Museum and in 1832, he was President of Trinity House in St Sepulchre Street. Tindall was made Mayor of the Borough for five terms of office - 1840 to 1841, 1841 to 1842, 1843 to 1844, 1846 to 1847 and 1849 to 1850. For many years, Tindall was a Justice of the Peace, both for Scarborough and for the North Riding. He was a member of the Piers and Harbours Commission and had been one of the Improvement Commissioners of the Town. In 1863, he was elected an Alderman for six years. However, declining health and frequent absences from the Town obliged him to resign in 1868, ending his municipal career.

Robert Tindall and his wife Ann had at least six children. Their Scarborough home was the *White House*, Long Westgate. However, in 1866, Robert also bought Kirby Misperton Hall, near Pickering from Captain Legard. As Robert got older, he spent more and more time there and, although a Quaker, he attended the local Anglican Church. In the early summer of 1871, because of increasing ill health, he returned to Scarborough to be near his doctor.

Robert Tindall died on 21 June 1871 at the *White House*, aged 81. His hearse was followed by eight carriages of family and servants and he was buried in the Quaker burial ground in St Sepulchre Street. He left a widow, Ann, two sons and four daughters. In 1880, his eldest child, Isabella Ann, married Joshua Rowntree (q.v.) in Ilkley.

Further reading
Scarborough Mercury 24 June 1871 (Obituary)

WALKER, Leasowe
1832 (Leeds) - post 1902

Mayor 1887-1888

Leasowe Walker was born on 9 August 1832, the son of Ard Walker of Thorner, five miles North-East of Leeds. Leasowe Walker was articled to a local solicitor but his father and mother both died before he qualified. He abandoned his legal studies to live the life of a country gentleman. During the season he made frequent visits to Scarborough where he met his wife and in 1873 the couple settled in the Town.

Leasowe Walker did not enter local politics but in 1886 was made a Justice of the Peace for the Borough. In November 1887, the Town Council were struggling to find a councillor or alderman willing to become Mayor for the period 1887 to 1888. It was decided to approach someone who was not a member of the Corporation. The mayoralty was offered to Lieutenant Colonel Steble (q.v.) but he declined. A special meeting of the Council was then convened and Leasowe Walker was proposed as an alternative candidate. The outgoing Mayor, John W. Woodall (q.v.), with other councillors, visited Walker with their proposal, which he accepted. He was the first non-member of the Town Council to become Mayor.

Leasowe Walker met Fanny Hall Robson, the daughter of John Robson of Durham, on a visit to Scarborough. In July 1873, they married at St Martin's-on-the-Hill, Scarborough and set up home in the Town living at *Morningside*, Grosvenor Road. They had one daughter, Kathleen born in 1875 and the family lived in Scarborough at least until 1902.

Further reading
Scarborough Gazette 10 November 1887 (Appointment as Mayor)
Scarborough Mercury 11 November 1887 (Appointment as Mayor)

WEDDELL, Thomas
1792 (York) - 1862 (Scarborough)
Mayor 1838-1839 and 1844-1845

Thomas Weddell was born in York in 1792. He studied medicine and qualified as a Licentiate of the Society of Apothecaries (LSA) and a Member of the Royal College of Surgeons (MRCS) in 1818 when he gave a Scarborough address, suggesting that he may have been apprenticed here. By 1821, he had settled in the Town as a surgeon, firstly in Newborough Street and later in Queen Street. About 1846, Thomas Weddell took Dr Richard Cross (q.v.) into partnership in the Queen Street practice. Weddell was also Surgeon to the Northern Sea-bathing Infirmary, to the Ordnance, to a detachment of the 6th Foot, and to the Royal Artillery, all in Scarborough. In 1854, Thomas Weddell

was elected an honorary Fellow of the Royal College of Surgeons of England (FRCS).

From about 1825, Dr Weddell was also co-proprietor, with Dr Thomas Thompson, of warm seawater baths (i.e. medicinal baths) in Quay Street near Scarborough harbour. After 1827, Weddell became the sole proprietor and by 1855 the business was significant enough to justify a full-time manager - Mr Robert Coates.

Weddell's Baths

Thomas Weddell was elected a councillor for the North Ward in the first municipal elections of 1836 and at the same time elected an Alderman for a term of six years. In 1838, he was made Mayor of the Borough for the period 1838 to 1839, being the fourth in line of Scarborough Mayors. He was again Mayor for the period 1844/45. He was also a local magistrate.

Thomas Weddell was a very popular Scarborough doctor and in 1860 his friends and patients commissioned a portrait of him which was published as a lithograph by the American lithographer, Napoleon Sarony, and sold in Scarborough.

Thomas Weddell married Caroline Williamson of Ripon and they had two daughters. Caroline Blanche, born 1841, married Frederick Pontifex of London in 1872 and Emily Maud, born 1844, married Thomas Luis Fernandez of Wakefield in 1870.

Thomas Weddell died at his Scarborough home, 7, Albion Place on 25 October 1862, aged 70. He was survived by his wife, Caroline. Her brother, Robert Williamson, Chairman of the York City and County Bank and a Director of the North Eastern Railway, died in Paris in December 1864 and Mrs Weddell then moved into Robert's house, *Esplanade Villa*, with her two daughters.

Further reading
Scarborough Gazette 4 & 18 November 1860 (Weddell's portrait)
Scarborough Gazette 13 November 1862 (Obituary, Town Council's tribute)

Bayliss, A & P, The Medical Profession in Scarborough, 1700 to 1899, Scarborough 2005 (Biography)

Power, Sir D'Arcy, Plarr's Lives of the Fellows of the Royal College of Surgeons of England, J Wright & Sons, Bristol, 1930

WHELDON, John
1808 (Hunmanby) - 1865 (Seamer)

Mayor 1856-1857

John Wheldon was born in 1808 at Hunmanby, 8 miles South of Scarborough. In the late-1830s, he and his family settled in Scarborough where he had a business as a corn miller and merchant. By 1851, he employed five men and two labourers, had one apprentice and owned 213 acres of land.

John Wheldon was elected an Alderman of the Borough and in November 1856 was made Mayor for the period 1856 to 1857.

John Wheldon and his wife Mary Ann had at least three children one son and two daughters. During his mayoral year one of his daughters, Sarah, married Rev. William Stacy Chapman of Amersham, at the Baptist Chapel in Scarborough. Another daughter, Mary Ann Clarke, married John Henry Eaton of Stamford at Seamer Parish Church, the service being performed by her brother-in-law Rev. W. S. Chapman. By 1881, their son, John, was keeper to the Costa Anglers' Club at Pickering.

In an 1855 directory, John Wheldon is listed as a farmer of North Marine Road, Scarborough. However, by 1857 he is recorded as a farmer in Seamer, a village 4 miles South-West of Scarborough.

John Wheldon died suddenly in November 1865, aged 58, at his home at Seamer. His widow, Mary Ann, died in 1873, also at Seamer.

WHITE, George
1817 (Portsea) - 1884 (Scarborough)

Mayor 1873-1874

George White was born in 1817 in Portsea. However, by the 1840s he was working in Scarborough as a manager for *Messrs Rowntree's* but soon afterwards he went into partnership with Robert Rennison, a draper of 32,

Newborough Street. By 1851, White described himself as a linen draper of 7, Cliff Bridge Terrace where his wife kept a lodging house. Four years later he was in business as a grocer and tea-dealer at 59, Newborough. He later developed the business to include wine and spirits and the sale of hats and of postage stamps. In 1870, he built additional premises at 1, Ramshill Road, which was also the family home. For a period of time, George White was also a restaurant contractor to Scarborough Spa, Scarborough Aquarium, the Victoria Rooms in Bridlington Quay and the Railway Stations at Mirfield, Halifax, Wakefield, Wigan and Sowerby Bridge.

Purveyor to H.M. the King of the Belgians and H.R.H. the Prince of Wales.

GEORGE WHITE,
WINE & SPIRIT MERCHANT,
Grocer and Italian Warehouseman,
1, RAMSHILL ROAD, SCARBOROUGH,
(Albion Crescent Post Office.)
AGENT FOR
Bass & Co.'s Burton Ales. Worthington & Co.'s India Pale Ale.
GUINNESS'S EXTRA DUBLIN STOUT.
WINES. CHAMPAGNES. SPIRITS.
TEAS, COFFEES, GENERAL GROCERIES,
Italian Goods, Provisions, &c.

This Establishment is very conveniently situated for supplying Visitors staying at the Esplanade, Esplanade Gardens, Prince of Wales Terrace, Albion Road, Crown Terrace, Crown Crescent, Cambridge Terrace, St. Martin's Square and Terrace, Grosvenor Terrace, &c., &c.

George White was elected to the Town Council in November 1862, representing the North Ward. He was made Mayor of the Borough for the period 1873 to 1874 and in that office was instrumental in bringing the Channel Fleet to Scarborough. In 1877, White was elected to represent Scarborough Corporation on the Harbour Commissioners' Board.

George White died on 27 May 1884, leaving a widow, Elizabeth, four daughters and one son, all unmarried. White was buried at Scarborough Cemetery after a funeral service given by the Baptist minister, Rev. R. I. Mesquitta.

Further reading
Scarborough Mercury 30 May 1884 (Obituary)

WHITTAKER, Thomas
1813 (Grindleton) - 1899 (Scarborough)

Mayor 1880-1881

Thomas Whittaker was born in 1813 in Grindleton, then in the West Riding of Yorkshire, one of eight boys and one girl. When he was ten years old the family moved to Lancashire living at various times in Preston, Blackburn and Bolton. In 1835, at the age of 22, after a lecture on temperance at the Theatre Royal, Blackburn, Thomas Whittaker took a pledge of abstinence from alcohol. From then on he devoted his life to the

Temperance Movement which at that time had its headquarters at Preston. From 1837 to 1845 he worked in London with Father Matthew and other reformers and went on to preach temperance throughout England, Ireland, Scotland and America.

Whittaker first visited Scarborough in January 1839 when he lectured on temperance at the Methodist Chapel, Church Stairs. In 1849, he came to reside permanently in the Town having been invited by William Rowntree (1806-1901) to become the proprietor of a Temperance Hotel in Newborough. In 1850, he was Vice-President of the Scarborough Temperance Society which included the Town's leading Quaker families, the Tindalls and the Rowntrees. Whittaker published two books on the subject of temperance and wrote articles under the pseudonym of *Watchman* in *The Express* but the periodical refused to publish his  work on the grounds that it was too dangerous. Undaunted, Whittaker ran his own paper, *The Watchman* between 1867 and 1869. In 1875, with a consortium of Liberals, he bought a local newspaper, the *Scarborough Mercury,* from E. T. W. Dennis. Shortly afterwards the Whittaker family, Thomas and his two sons, became sole proprietors of the *Mercury.* In 1882, they launched the *Scarborough Evening News* which remained in the family until 1986, when the titles were sold to East Midlands Allied Press by Thomas Whittaker's great-great-grandson Paul.

Thomas Whittaker, a Liberal, began his involvement with local politics in Scarborough in the 1850s. In 1855 there was agreement in the Town that a new burial ground was urgently needed. The Anglicans, represented by Rev. John Whiteside, Vicar of Scarborough, argued for a separate cemetery for the Church of England while Whittaker successfully argued that the cemetery should be non-denominational. However, the cemetery chapel was designed with a separate area for the established church. Thomas Whittaker made several attempts to be elected to the Town Council but was unsuccessful, mainly because of his outspoken criticism of many aspects of municipal life. He was finally elected in January 1867 but defeated in 1873. He was successful in a by-election in 1876 and remained a councillor until 1884 when he retired. Thomas Whittaker was made Mayor of the Borough for the period 1880 to 1881 at which time he was appointed a Justice of the Peace. In July 1893, the British Temperance League, at its annual conference in York, acknowledged Thomas Whittaker's lifetime services to the movement. He was presented with several gifts and an illuminated address signed by the League's President, W. S. Caine (q.v.), who had been Scarborough's MP from 1880 to 1885.

Thomas Whittaker was married three times. He first married at the age of 19 in 1832 while living in Glossop, but his wife died in 1837. The following year he married Louisa, but this *union was broken in January 1875 when he was on a visit to the United States.* In 1879, he married Augusta Green of Devizes who died in September 1898. Two of Thomas Whittaker's sons by his wife Louisa, Meredith Thompson and Thomas Palmer both became Scarborough councillors. They ran an iron foundry and ironmongery in the Town and were both involved with the management of the family newspapers. T. P. Whittaker moved to London and in 1892 was elected MP for Spen Valley. Meredith, later Sir Meredith Whittaker, was Mayor of Scarborough for two terms of office from 1919 to 1921.

Thomas Whittaker died at his home, 1, Belgrave Terrace on 20 November 1899. There was a funeral service at Westborough Wesleyan Chapel and he was buried in Scarborough Cemetery. His funeral was reported to have been the largest seen in Scarborough *for many years* being attended by *all shades of political and social life in Scarborough.* Many members of the Temperance Movement came, and an address was given by William S. Caine.

Further reading
Scarborough Mercury 24 November 1899 (Obituary)
Scarborough Evening News, Supplement, 14 July 2007 (History of the Scarborough Evening News 1882-2007)
Binns, Jack, Heroes, Rogues and Eccentrics, A Biographical Journey Through Scarborough's Past, Blackthorn Press, 2002 pgs 175-182 (biography)
Blakey, J.W. (ed.) Some Scarborough Faces, Past and Present, Scarborough Gazette Printing & Publishing Co. 1901 pgs 28-34 (Biography)

WILLIAMSON, Joseph
1832 (Scarborough) - 1896 (Scarborough)

Mayor 1872-1873

Joseph Williamson was born in Scarborough on 6 January 1832. He began his career as a grocer, tea and coffee merchant in the Town. However, by 1862 he was proprietor of the Bull Commercial and Family Hotel, Posting House and Livery Stables in Westborough. In 1869, he moved to become proprietor of the prestigious Crown Hotel, Esplanade where he remained until well into the 1890s.

Joseph Williamson first entered local politics in 1865 when he was elected as councillor for the North Ward. He was re-elected in November 1868 and returned unopposed in November 1871. He was made Mayor of the Borough for the period 1872 to 1873. In his year of office the first sod of the Scarborough-Whitby Railway line was turned and two new schools were opened in Scarborough under the new Education Act - Falsgrave Infants' School and the Central Board School. In September 1873, Leopold II, King of the Belgians, made a private visit to Scarborough. At the end of his mayoralty, Joseph Williamson was elected Alderman, a position he held until 1892. During his time as a local councillor he held various municipal posts, including being a member of the Burial Board.

CROWN HOTEL,

ESPLANADE,

SCARBOROUGH,

CONTIGUOUS TO THE SPA,

SANDS,

CLIFF BRIDGE,

AND

PLEASURE GROUNDS.

JOSEPH WILLIAMSON,

Proprietor.

Joseph Williamson was twice married. In December 1852, he married Hannah Taylor, the sister-in-law of George White (q.v.). Hannah and Joseph had a large number of children many dying in infancy and Hannah died at the age of 44, in 1876. Their four surviving sons Richard, William, Harry and Sidney all qualified in medicine. Sidney was Resident House Surgeon at Scarborough Hospital and Dispensary from 1888 to 1889. Joseph Williamson married for a second time in 1878 to Mary Elizabeth Hallaway of Carlisle.

Joseph Williamson sold the Crown Hotel in the early 1890s and moved to live at 1, Ramshill Road, with his sister-in-law Mrs George White.

Joseph Williamson died at his home on 4 April 1896, aged 64 and was interred in the family vault at Scarborough Cemetery after a funeral service at Christ Church.

Further reading
Scarborough Gazette 9 April 1896 (Obituary)
The Crown Hotel Scarborough, 150 Years of Hospitality, 1995
Scarborough Library ref no. 647.9442 (History of the Crown Hotel)

WILLIS, George
1801 (Scarborough) - 1873 (Scarborough)

Mayor 1854-1855

George Willis was born in Scarborough in 1801 into a shipping family. From March 1826 to April 1829 he was master of the ship *Europe* and from 1825 until 1847 he was part owner of at least seven vessels. He described himself as a ship-owner in the 1851 census.

Sometime before November 1854, George Willis was made an Alderman. In that month James Tindall was chosen to be Mayor of the Borough but refused to accept the office and was fined £25 for so doing. George Willis was made Mayor in his place for the period 1854 to 1855.

George Willis never married. He lived at 3, York Place, Scarborough where he died on 23 September 1873. He was buried at St Mary's Parish Church on 27 September.

WOODALL, John
1801 (Scarborough) - 1879 (Scarborough)

Mayor 1851-1852

John Woodall was born in Scarborough on 25 October 1801, the eldest son of John and Ann Woodall. John Woodall jun. went to sea on board a vessel belonging to his uncle Richard Wilson, the founder of the Mariners' Asylum in Castle Road. At the age of 21, Woodall was given command of the brig *Arab*, one of the fastest vessels of her day, which was trading to Smyrna. While at sea, he acquired a knowledge of foreign languages and, it was said, a love of art. In 1832, Woodall's grandfather, who had been one of the four founders of Scarborough's *Old Bank* in 1788, died. John Woodall's father had become a partner in the Bank in 1824 and on the death of his grandfather, John junior was admitted as a partner. The

Woodall family owned a considerable amount of land in and around Scarborough and by 1871 John Woodall was estimated to own 1,388 acres of land with a gross estimated rental of £5,305.

As his father and grandfather before him, John Woodall was both a junior and a senior bailiff before the Municipal Corporation Act 1835. He was the only member of the old Corporation elected to the new Council in 1836 (see Introduction). Woodall was made Mayor of the Borough for the period 1851 to 1852 and on his  retirement he presented the Corporation with a ceremonial gold chain which has been worn by Scarborough's Mayors ever since. John Woodall was a Conservative in politics but it was said that he became more liberal in later years.

Woodall held a number of public appointments. He was a Commissioner of Piers and Harbours, Chairman of Scarborough Water Company, a Deputy Lieutenant for the North Riding of Yorkshire and a Justice of the Peace for the North and East Ridings. However, he rejected an offer to become a Borough magistrate and also refused to consider standing for Parliament. In 1866, John Woodall was Chairman of the Board of Guardians when a lugger, *St Joseph* that had arrived from Fécamp, Normandy was found to have cholera amongst its crew. Being concerned about the likely adverse effect on visitors to Scarborough, Woodall agreed that the sick could be nursed to health in secret in the workhouse infirmary. The dead were buried discretely in the disused Quaker graveyard in Westover Road (then Folly Lane). The presence of the Frenchmen in the Town only came to light later when a French Man-of-War came to Scarborough to convey the thanks of the fishermen of Fécamp together with a commemorative plaque.

John Woodall married his cousin, Mary Eleanor, daughter of Rev. W. Woodall, rector of Branston and Waltham, Leicestershire. They had three sons and four daughters. The eldest son was John Woodall Woodall (q.v.), their second son, Charles William, became a barrister and joined the Bank shortly before his father's death, while the third, Edward Henry, took an MA degree at Oriel College, Oxford. John Woodall's eldest daughter, Mary Hebden, married John Dent Dent (q.v.) who was Liberal MP for Scarborough for sixteen years. Another daughter, Louisa, married Rev. A.

111

W. Headlam, vicar of St Oswald's, Durham. Woodall's other two daughters, Edith Jane (1838-1921) and Augusta (1844-1924) did not marry. Augusta was active in public life in Scarborough, especially in connection with the Hospital and Dispensary of which she was a Life Governor and a Member and Chairwoman of its Ladies' Committee. She was also an accomplished artist.

. John Woodall died on 13 February 1879 at his home *St Nicholas House*, today Scarborough's Town Hall. A funeral service was held by Archdeacon Blunt at Seamer, where Woodall was buried in the family grave. The Mayor, W. C. Land (q.v.), had asked that all shops and other places of business in Scarborough closed from 10am to noon. A memorial service was held the following Sunday at Scarborough Parish Church with the Mayor and Corporation in formal attendance and a muffled peel of bells was rung at close of the service. His widow, Mary Eleanor, died on 8 March 1883.

Further reading
Scarborough Gazette 13 February 1879 (Obituary)
Scarborough Pictorial 11 February 1914 (Biography)
Baker, Joseph Brogden, The History of Scarborough, London, 1882 pgs 452-453 (Biography)
Phillips, Maberly, History of Banks, Bankers and Banking, Northumberland, Durham & North Yorkshire, 1755-1894, London 1894 Pg 196 (History of the Bank) Pg 198 (Biography)

WOODALL, John Woodall
1831 (Scarborough) - 1905 (London)
Mayor 1868-1869, 1881-1882, 1886 & 1886-1887

John Woodall Woodall was born on 3 December 1831, the eldest son of John Woodall (q.v.) and his wife Mary. J. W. Woodall was educated at Rugby School and Oriel College, Oxford where he obtained a first class degree in Natural Science in 1854. He served in the militia during the Crimean War (1853-56) and returned to Scarborough in 1857. In 1862, he became a partner in the family bank which had been founded in Scarborough by his great-grandfather and three other investors in 1788. It was amalgamated with Barclay's Bank in 1896. Besides being active in the Bank and a significant local landowner, J. W. Woodall was a Fellow of the Geographical Society and a Fellow of the Zoological Society. He carried out extensive research into the North Sea fisheries from a series of yachts that he had built and fitted out as marine laboratories. On occasions he

placed his vessel at the disposal of the East Coast Fisheries Board which had no money to purchase its own vessel. Woodall was a strong advocate of the artificial breeding programmes for sea-fish that had been developed in Norway and he published various articles on the subject. In 1894, he commissioned the building of an exhibition hall on Scarborough's Foreshore that could accommodate 5,000 people. Here he organised a major sea-fisheries exhibition covering every imaginable aspect of fishing. It was formally opened on 31 May 1895 by General Sir Evelyn Wood VC, Prime Warden of the Fishmongers' Company. Woodall was a keen yachtsman being a member of both the Royal Yorkshire and the Royal Thames Yacht Clubs and he was an honorary lieutenant in the Royal Naval Reserve.

J. W. Woodall was an active freemason, being a founder member of the *Denison Lodge* and the *Leopold Lodge* in Scarborough as well as being a member of the *Royal Lodge*. As early as 1867, he was described as *one of the most active Freemasons that Scarborough has ever known* and in 1885 he was elected Grand Treasurer, the first provincial mason to attain that honour. His regalia were donated to the freemasons in Scarborough at his death and displayed in library of the Masonic Hall.

John W. Woodall was elected a member of the Town Council for the North Ward in 1863 and retained a seat until 1889. He was made Mayor for the period 1868-1869 and in 1870 he was made an Alderman. He was again made Mayor for the period 1881-1882. In June 1886 when the Mayor, Joshua Rowntree (q.v.), resigned to contest a Parliamentary election, Woodall took his place for the rest of the year and was made Mayor again for the following period, 1886-1887. He retired from Scarborough Council in 1889 but in the same year he was elected to the newly formed County Council as a Liberal representative for Scarborough's Central Ward.

Amongst various other appointments, John W. Woodall was a director of the Electric Supply Company, a member of the Committee of the Cliff Bridge Company and a large shareholder in both the North Promenade Pier Company and in the North Cliff Tramway Company.

John Woodall Woodall lived in the family home, *St Nicholas House*, until 1898 when he sold the house, gardens and exhibition hall to Scarborough Corporation. *St Nicholas House* became the present day Scarborough Town Hall, his gardens formed St Nicholas Cliff public gardens and the exhibition hall became Olympia, an all-weather tourist attraction until its destruction by fire in 1975.

John Woodall Woodall married late in life and after the sale he and his wife moved to London where he continued to be active in Masonic life. He died suddenly at his London home, *Queen's Mansions*, Victoria Street, on 21 March 1905, aged 73, leaving a widow.

Further reading
Scarborough Gazette 14 March, 16 May & 6 June 1895 (Woodall's Exhibition Hall)
Scarborough Mercury 23 March 1905 (Obituary)
Blakey, J.W. (ed.) Some Scarborough Faces, Past and Present, Scarborough Gazette Printing & Publishing Co. 1901 pgs 22-26 (Biography)
Phillips, Maberly, History of Banks, Bankers and Banking, Northumberland, Durham & North Yorkshire, 1755-1894, London 1894 Pg 196 (History of the Bank) Pg 198 (Biography)